Jesse,

Life can be a
Full Circle + we
Are Fortunate to
Have You As Our Lawyer.

MW00815096

CHIP MERLIN

MAVERICKS &MERLINS

SAILORS AND RENEGADES LEAVE SHORE

WHAT ABOUT YOU?

Advantage.

Published by Advantage, Charleston, South Carolina.
Member of Advantage Media Group.

ADVANTAGE is a registered trademark, and the Advantage colophon is a trademark of Advantage Media Group, Inc.

Printed in the United States of America.

10 9 8 7 6 5 4 3 2 1

ISBN: 978-1-64225-122-7
LCCN: 2020915304

Layout design by Wesley Strickland.

This publication is designed to provide accurate and authoritative information in regard to the subject matter covered. It is sold with the understanding that the publisher is not engaged in rendering legal, accounting, or other professional services. If legal advice or other expert assistance is required, the services of a competent professional person should be sought.

Advantage Media Group is proud to be a part of the Tree Neutral® program. Tree Neutral offsets the number of trees consumed in the production and printing of this book by taking proactive steps such as planting trees in direct proportion to the number of trees used to print books. To learn more about Tree Neutral, please visit **www.treeneutral.com**.

Advantage Media Group is a publisher of business, self-improvement, and professional development books and online learning. We help entrepreneurs, business leaders, and professionals share their Stories, Passion, and Knowledge to help others Learn & Grow. Do you have a manuscript or book idea that you would like us to consider for publishing? Please visit **advantagefamily.com** or call **1.866.775.1696**.

*To the members of all race committees who have
volunteered their time to allow me and my friends to
compete against each other in the sport we love.*

*"I far prefer the sensation of going fast to the
sensation of being handed a trophy."*

—Bill Lee, yacht designer and builder

*"I find the great thing in this world is not so much where
we stand, as in what direction we are moving: To reach
the port of heaven, we must sail sometimes with the
wind and sometimes against it—but we must sail,
and not drift, nor lie at anchor."*

—Oliver Wendell Holmes Sr.

*"I never quit. I've got a bunch of flags on my boat,
but there ain't no white flags. I don't surrender.
That's the story of my life."*

—Ted Turner

CONTENTS

FOREWORD

BOATS LIKE *MERLIN* don't just exist for one time, but for all time. As a young sailor, I can remember seeing and hearing about this sled that defied expectations and performance. Bill Lee's revolutionary design ushered in a new era of racing. The boat's performance throughout the following forty years showcases the power of design and the passion that Lee crafted into the soul of *Merlin.*

I first encountered Chip Merlin in Newport with some friends. He was excited as all get-out about the upcoming Newport to Bermuda Race, and he seemed genuinely happy about the sailing and, of course, owning and sailing the legendary *Merlin.* I wished him and his crew the best of luck on their race. Chip's enthusiasm for *Merlin* popped up again when I happened upon him in *Sail* magazine. He is an old-school owner in a new-school world. His sense of respect and value for his crew and for his vessel is evident.

Recently, I was able to see the newly renovated *Merlin* in all her glory in the latest running of the Transpac. She is both a vessel returned to her glory and an evolved machine with all the bells, whistles, and adaptations to make her truly a contemporary ocean racer.

Chip and his boat are two Merlins that have been, and will continue to be, serious contenders in our sailing world and beyond.

—**Ken Read,** President of North Sails

PREFACE

IN NOVEMBER 1978, when I was nineteen and an undergraduate studying business administration at the University of Florida, I read an article in *Sports Illustrated* about a revolutionary offshore racing sailboat that had won the Transpacific Yacht Race the previous year. The Transpac, as the race is called, consists of a mostly downwind jaunt of 2,225 nautical miles from Long Beach, California, to Honolulu, Hawaii. Begun in 1906, the Transpac is one of the oldest organized ocean yacht races in America.

In 1977, the winner had come to the racecourse by the most extraordinary set of circumstances. The yacht's name was *Merlin*. Since my last name is Merlin, and I like wizards, I was naturally drawn to the story.

I was also a longtime "one-design" racer, mostly Flying Scots, a traditionally built nineteen-foot racing sloop. (In one-design racing, as opposed to handicap racing, all the boats are of the same design, so the first vessel to the finish wins.) In fact, I'd racked up a host of wins on Chesapeake Bay during the previous summer after racing passionately and successfully during my teenage years. Sailboat racing was in my blood, though by November 1978 my focus had shifted from boats to my undergraduate studies, and to my burgeoning desire to go to law school.

As I read about *Merlin* and her Santa Cruz–based designer and builder, Bill Lee, it seemed as if the story was a work of fiction rather than fact. According to the article, Bill had built the boat in an old chicken coop, practically going broke in the process, and had gone on to win the 1977 Transpac, just as he'd intended.

Bill Lee also set an elapsed-speed record for the race that stood for twenty years. Bill's revolutionary design, known as an ultralight displacement boat, or ULDB, started a trend in offshore racing sailboats that continues today. I still vividly recall shaking my head and vowing that I'd buy *Merlin* if I ever had the means.

Thirty-nine years later, I did just that.

Merlin is a custom-built racing sloop that really shook up the racing scene on the West Coast when she was first launched. She's seventy-one feet overall from the tip of her stubby bowsprit to her sugar-scoop stern. She has a beam of only twelve feet. That's thin for a yacht of her length. In fact, various writers have called her a "pencil," a "sliver," and a "dart." My crew calls her a "monocat." That's a nod to the fact that she's so skinny in width that it's almost as if she is half a catamaran, only she doesn't need the second hull to stay upright in a stiff breeze because she has a needlelike, lead-ballasted keel that juts down eleven feet below the waterline. She only displaces 24,000 pounds, or less than half the weight of most boats her size.

At the time she set the Transpac record in 1977, there was nothing like her in the world. People even thought she was dangerous. She was no more dangerous than any other offshore racing yacht, of course, but anything new tends to spook some people. I guess that's just human nature, but being scared of the new has never made sense to me. To be sure, a sailboat that can get up on plane and sail at over twenty knots is *still* something to behold on the racecourse. Back then, it was simply spectacular, the buzz of the West Coast racing community, and soon the talk of the entire racing world. *Merlin* has stayed a well-known commodity, having won the Transpac three times, as well as a host of other races.

I lost track of *Merlin* after college. I plunged headfirst into the law and never looked back. But the boat popped up on my radar screen big time in 2017 in a strange confluence of events that ultimately changed my life. The first link in the chain was Bill Lee.

After regaining possession of the yacht, Bill raced in the 2017 Transpac. The race was a personal celebration for him, marking the fortieth anniversary of the boat's first Transpac win. By coincidence, I'd just gotten back into sailboat racing in 2017, so I naturally paid attention to *Merlin*'s progress. She didn't win the race, but she did beat her old record time, which pleased Bill to no end. He put the boat up for sale after the race. I'd been nursing the idea of taking my dad, who was my first sailing mentor, on the Newport-Bermuda race in 2018, and I'd been looking for a suitable yacht to charter for the adventure.

I learned that chartering a yacht for offshore racing is not a game for the faint of wallet. With a growing sense of urgency to find a boat, as the start was approaching fast, I was astonished and thrilled that *Merlin* came up for sale just when I was looking for a boat like her to sail to Bermuda with Dad. I ditched the charter idea and instead bought the boat. Appropriately enough, the Bermuda race coincided with Father's Day, and I was able to make a couple of my dreams come true. I was able to buy a boat I had only dreamed of owning, and I was able to take my dad on the race to Bermuda, bringing him full circle back to the days of his youth, when he ran the race twice in the mid-1950s.

How often in life do you get the chance to act on your dreams? I believe that these opportunities exist almost regardless of what your dreams are. The idea is to *act*, not to just fantasize. There are always excuses not to pursue what you really want to do. Fear of failure, a lack of vision, an overriding sense of inertia—that and much more can keep you locked into inaction or negativity about what you can do to lead a happier and more purposeful life. Changes will come, regardless of whether they're the ones you sought. If you dare to dream, and you dare to dream big, look at those dreams optimistically as chances for happiness. If you take action to methodically turn those dreams into reality, you may find that you'll achieve more than you ever thought possible.

Working toward something gives us purpose in life, gives us hope, and opens up a realm of limitless possibilities. Think about Bill Lee. He hatched an idea for a revolutionary boat in a chicken coop, and then he did what it took to turn plans on the drawing board into a race-winning yacht. People thought he was crazy. He shrugged and went about his business.

> Moving forward with fair winds and calm seas can open the very horizon to limitless possibilities. All you have to do is set your course and go.

The tang of salt in the air, the feel of spray on your face as the boat surges through the waves, and the sheer thrill of getting the most speed possible through proper sail trim and expert helmsmanship are what make sailboat racing so much fun, especially on a big offshore speedster like *Merlin*. Without fun, what's the point of life? Why go through life like a robot? Why go through it as if it's a dress rehearsal? We only get one shot at life. We might as well have a good and purposeful time while we're here. Bill Lee says, "Fast is fun!" I couldn't agree with him more. Fast is really fun, especially on a racing yacht like *Merlin*.

In a sense, that's why I decided to write this book. It's an homage to the yacht *Merlin*, and to the man who designed and built her. It's the story of how I came to own and successfully race one of the most iconic racing yachts in American history. But mostly, the book is about having the courage to follow your dreams, no matter what those dreams are. Success, regardless of how you define it, does not come from staying in place. Success comes from following through, regardless of whether you fail or not. If you do fail, there are other paths you can follow to fulfill other dreams, if you aren't afraid to keep trying. But the dreams you have now are what matter. Moving forward with fair winds and calm seas can open the very horizon to limitless possibilities. All you have to do is set your course and go.

1

INSPIRED

I STOOD AT THE HELM of *Patience* and guided her over the starting line in fairly good order. I'd had plenty of practice with starts in the small one-design sailboats I'd raced off and on since I was a kid. I'd just never steered a fifty-four-foot cruising boat across the line in an offshore ocean race. My friend Dave Kilcoyne, who owns *Patience*, had never started a sailboat race before. This was all completely novel for him as well.

Starting a race requires crossing an imaginary starting line just as the gun goes off. If you time it wrong and cross before the gun fires, you've got to go back and do it all over again. Bad starts lose races, whether you're on a one-design or some other kind of boat. Every second would count on a course that, as the crow flies, would be just over 280 nautical miles almost due south from Tampa Bay to Morro Castle at the entrance to Havana Harbor. Unlike in a short-duration one-design race, you've got a lot of time to play with as the race progresses. That means there's plenty of time to goof up, or to shine.

I wanted to get the start right. I don't believe in half efforts. If you're not all in at 100 percent, don't even bother to go for it.

We could feel the excitement among the six of us who were aboard. Of the crew, only one sailor among us, Brian Malone, had any kind of ocean racing experience. I'd just recently met Brian in preparation for the race. He's the owner of North Sails Gulf Coast, Inc. His outfit made the spinnaker for *Patience*. He's a great guy and a stellar seaman, and I was grateful to have him along.

The St. Petersburg Yacht Club had capped the fleet for the St. Petersburg–Habana race at eighty boats. I'm not sure if every entry showed up, but whatever the actual number, there sure were a lot of boats bopping around just before the starting line, jockeying for the best position relative to the wheezing light southwesterly breeze that barely rippled the water. An Irwin 54 displaces 46,000 pounds unloaded. Dave had packed the boat for comfortable cruising, which had added considerable weight. He'd even added a washer and dryer! The yacht is super heavy compared to an ultralight displacement boat like *Merlin*. *Patience* needs a fairly stiff breeze to move her at anything close to maximum hull speed, and her weight doesn't help. She has a center cockpit with a full cockpit enclosure: basically a plastic shelter to keep the crew out of the weather. Problem is, those things cause tremendous windage. In other words, they can act like a sail. In this case, it contributed to our slow lope across the starting line.

The fleet began to separate as we headed toward the mouth of Tampa Bay, eking out every bit of boat speed that we could manage, given the conditions. I could tell this was totally awesome for Dave. As a "cruiser," in general he doesn't focus on sailing the boat for optimal speed. Few cruisers do that. They generally value comfort over speed; I like to go fast. I like to get out there, win the race, and then go back to doing what I love, which is fighting for the little guy in court against insurance companies that don't want to pay up.

"Hey, I want to do some skippering," Dave said.

I grinned. He was like a little kid, though he's just a bit older than I am. I've known Dave since my days at the University of Florida. We were both frat boys, hung in the same circles, and were involved in student government. I stood aside and gave Dave the helm. At this point, the fleet was stopped dead.

"I think we're sailing backward," I said.

We all looked over the side to see what the water was doing. Simultaneously, we took visual bearings on landmarks ashore to see which way we were going. Sure enough, *Patience* was sailing backward. Literally losing ground. The incoming tide, though not terribly strong, was enough to put the boat on course to return to the St. Petersburg Yacht Club … stern first.

"I think we should consider dropping anchor," Brian said.

We all agreed that sounded sensible. If you can't move forward, at least stop slipping backward. In business, if you're losing ground, you can usually take some action to mitigate the setback, or to actually reverse it. The same goes for sailing. In our case, we dropped the anchor and waited for the wind to strengthen. And, lo and behold, the breeze did pick up a little. We upped anchor and got going.

At this point, some of you might be wondering why in the world a bunch of sailboats would be racing to Cuba in 2017. That's a fair

> In business, if you're losing ground, you can usually take some action to mitigate the setback, or to actually reverse it. The same goes for sailing.

enough question, since relations between our countries have not been cordial. The answer starts with President Barack Obama.

In 2016, Obama figured that it was about time for the United States to thaw the frost between America and Cuba, a cold spell that had begun in 1959 when Fidel Castro and his pals ousted the corrupt government led by Fulgencio Batista after two years of bloody conflict. The revolution erupted in large part due to economic inequality, a theme that should be quite familiar to Americans these days. Indeed, Batista was in bed with big American business, selling off sugar plantations to the highest bidders. At one point, US and other foreign businesses owned more than 70 percent of Cuba's arable land. Of course, all that changed under the communist system. The state took control of virtually everything, though the Cuban people didn't benefit.

I played a very minor role in the thaw when a friend invited me to participate in a meeting in Washington, DC, with Cuban officials and a delegation from St. Petersburg, Florida, regarding how to move forward in an effort to mend fences between the two countries. The city of St. Petersburg and the capital of Cuba, Havana, had enjoyed warm commercial relations prior to 1959.

I was invited to the meeting because local political friends had set the meeting up, and because I had long known about the close relationship Port Tampa Bay had had with Cuba in the past. I wasn't a key player in the meeting, but it was interesting to see how everybody just wanted to move forward together to work for a better future for both nations. I liked being part of that, even if it was just a tiny part.

In 1883, the entrepreneur Henry B. Plant pushed his narrow-gauge railroad to the bay, opening up the easy transportation of goods to and from the port. That same year, phosphates were discovered in the Bone Valley southeast of Tampa, which fanned the rapid growth of what was formerly a small town out in the middle of nowhere. Two years later, Vicente Martinez-Ybor, a cigar-manufacturing magnate, moved his operations from Key West to Tampa, and more growth followed. Tobacco imports from Cuba through the port fueled a cigar-rolling industry that put Tampa on the map as the cigar-manufacturing capital of the world, at least for a time. Commercial fishing was also an important industry in the environs of Tampa Bay.

At the meeting, we briefly discussed reviving the St. Petersburg–Habana yacht race. The race was one of the most important and prestigious yacht races in the United States up until the Cuban Revolution, when the regatta was discontinued for obvious reasons. The race was the brainchild of George S. Gandy Jr., an avid sailor from a prominent St. Petersburg family. In 1929, after the stock market crashed in October, he sailed from St. Petersburg to Havana to get away from it all.

The Cuban capital was a popular destination for Americans at the time. Prohibition was in full swing. It's no surprise that wealthy Americans flocked to Havana to party. Gandy, or "Gidge," as he was nicknamed, was no exception. As he hung around Havana hobnobbing with other members of high society, he dreamed up the idea of starting a race that would run from the St. Petersburg Yacht Club to Cuba as a way to promote St. Pete businesses. Fostering additional business relationships between St. Pete and Cuba became all the more important once the United States began to slip into the Great Depression.

The first St. Petersburg–Habana race (the yacht club uses the Spanish spelling for Havana) began the following year on March 30, 1930, with eleven boats starting just off the St. Petersburg Municipal Pier. Over time, the race would attract some of the best yachts in the country, and the world. Thousands of spectators gathered to watch the start of the races, the beautiful wooden yachts with their colorful sails captivating onlookers. The race ranked among the top events in yachting. It was a real shame to have it stopped because of politics.

Ironically, four days before I was born in 1959, thirty-seven boats entered the St. Petersburg–Habana race. Fidel Castro had fully taken over in January. When the yachts arrived in Havana, there were reports of gunfire. Clearly, the unrest had continued even after Castro was in charge, and the yachties were a bit nervous about returning to Havana. Relations between Cuba and the United States went way downhill, as a result of the botched Bay of Pigs invasion in April 1961 and the Cuban Missile Crisis in October 1962. No more yacht races to Cuba.

Everything changes, though. In 2016, it looked like the thaw was really on between the United States and Cuba. But as of this writing, the Donald J. Trump administration has rescinded many of Obama's liberalizing policies regarding Cuba. Private recreational vessels can't legally go to Cuba anymore … again. No more yacht races to Cuba, at least for now. And that's a bloody shame, just as it was the first time.

At any rate, I was reading the newspaper back in 2016 when I saw that the race had been officially reinstated. Since I'd been in on one of the meetings to work out how to promote events between Cuba and the United States, I was interested in the story. The race would be good for the city, the yachting community, and the Cuban people. As it turned out, the race really did help St. Pete, bringing in just over an estimated $676,000 in economic activity from the 675 or so sailors who'd descended on the city for the race, according to the St. Petersburg Sailing Center. The sailors hailed from South Africa, the United Kingdom, Canada, France, Germany, the Netherlands, Spain, and the United States.

That same afternoon, I got a call from Dave Kilcoyne.

"You want to sail to Cuba?" he asked. "You know … in the big race?"

I'd been sailing intermittently for years, racing Flying Scots and other small sailboats. As a kid, I was a diehard sailor, but I'd given up sailing for the most part. I was busy growing Merlin Law Group. Sailing wasn't a big priority. It was fun, but not an obsession. I'd never sailed offshore before, much less raced a big boat, so the idea intrigued me.

Dave's Irwin 54 is a keel-centerboard sloop built for pleasure cruising and slow adventure, not racing. He's got her outfitted with all the creature comforts you could ever want. Dave's boat is basically a Winnebago with a stick. She's got a refrigerator, freezer, air conditioner, two showers, a wine cellar, TV, and so much more. I've already mentioned the washer and dryer. I'd never seen the boat, but Dave talked a lot about her. I knew she wouldn't be a rocket ship. Still …

I asked Dave if he had a spinnaker, knowing he probably didn't. I was right. He didn't. I told him we had to get a spinnaker, and that we needed an experienced ocean racer or two to come with us to show us the ropes. He said he knew just the guy: a sailmaker and ocean racer named Brian Malone. I said that sounded cool. I said I'd go.

The four-lane Bob Graham Sunshine Skyway Bridge connects St. Petersburg to Terra Ceia. It's a beautiful cable-suspension bridge that crosses the mouth of Tampa Bay. The fleet came together at the chokepoint in the channel going under the bridge. Dave remained at the helm, and we talked him through how to avoid collisions as we trimmed the sails in the continued light air. Although I won't get into it here, just understand that there are rules that say which boat has to give way when overtaking, crossing, or approaching from opposite directions. In theory, the rules keep you from colliding on a crowded racecourse, but accidents do happen, especially if you don't know the rules of the road, which Dave didn't.

After we sailed under the bridge, we continued slowly—oh, so ... so slowly—out the channel to the Gulf of Mexico. I'd sailed small boats on the ocean before, but always near land. I'm a bay and sound kind of guy, not a blue-water Sinbad the Sailor who tends to get shipwrecked a lot. What I was seeing of the ocean was nothing new to me. The broad blue expanse of the Gulf of Mexico spread out before me. Long low groundswells sloshed us around. It wasn't comfortable, and I wondered what I had gotten myself into.

Before the race, we'd consulted with a weather-routing service. Winds were expected to be light and variable for the next three days or so, with a strong frontal passage expected to come in after that. It was now February 28. The race was set to end March 5. Maybe, just maybe, we'd get there if the wind increased. The weather-routing service suggested that we sail west-southwest, with our bow pointed toward Mexico, as opposed to sailing the direct route almost due south to Havana. We were in search of the Loop Current, which essentially flows into the Gulf of Mexico and circles around and around in a never-ending motion. If we hit the Loop, we figured we could ride the river in the sea south at three to four knots. Would this tactic really work? None of us knew.

Later, I found out that a number of skippers and friends following the race online were surprised to see us depart from the bulk of the fleet on that westerly course to Mexico when everyone else was headed to Cuba. We struck off on our own with the knowledge that we probably would have to think outside the box if we were to stand any chance of winning. It takes courage to go do something out of the usual, to follow the path less traveled, or not traveled at all. This ties into the idea of change, which is present in everything we ever do in our personal and professional lives, whether we like it or not. Pursuing a path that you know will result in change and a venture into the unknown takes courage. Sometimes, you just have to be willing to take a logical, smart, and yet risky step, regardless of the outcome. Sometimes you have to sail to Mexico to get to Cuba.

The experience of ocean racing was turning out to be something rather different from what I'd envisioned. As the day progressed, we sailed farther and farther offshore. Now, that was something different for me. The ocean is really big. You lose sight of land, then you lose sight of all the other boats, and you're out there alone, having to rely on your boat and your wits to get where you want to go. The slow-motion ride continued as the sun set, and it continued on into the night. We settled into our watch schedule. We didn't expect to hit the Loop Current until the next day. We couldn't get there soon enough, in my book. I dislike sailing in little or no wind. You get nowhere fast doing that.

After midnight, I was at the helm chatting with Dave's sister, Jackie. The stars looked so close and so bright that it was as if I could reach up and pluck them from the heavens. There's something magical about stargazing from the deck of a sailboat slowly making its way through a sea that's as black as the inside of a cave, the gentle breeze soft on your cheek, the sound of the hull parting the water, a trail of firefly-green phosphorescence astern in the wake. I'd never experienced anything like it, and it awakened in me a desire to explore the world of bigger boats. As a middle-aged guy, I felt a little like a kid again.

"Oh, my God! We're taking on water!" one of my companions said from down below.

"We're what?" I asked.

"We're sinking!"

Oh, great! We're sinking in the middle of the Gulf of Mexico, I thought.

"I think we should turn on the bilge pump," I said.

All the serenity went … *poof!* Brian, who was off watch, leaped out of his bunk to see what was happening. I didn't panic. None of us did. We wouldn't die if we sank, not in those placid conditions. And we had a life raft, of course. But we really didn't want to sink. It would certainly have ruined Dave's day. Brian eventually narrowed down the source of the leak to the air conditioner.

But we at first all thought the leak originated from the centerboard. An Irwin 54 has a keel that extends down into the water and a centerboard that passes through the keel, which give the boat a deeper draft. A deeper draft gives you better tracking ability, especially when sailing close to the wind. The centerboard option lets you nose into shallow harbors, if you raise the board. Essentially, you get the best of both worlds. All day and night, we'd been wondering if the centerboard was up or down. We wanted it down, but we weren't sure if it was down because the mechanical apparatus that raised and lowered the board wasn't working properly.

While Brian did his troubleshooting, I stayed on the helm. I wasn't looking at the stars anymore. I was straining to hear what was going on down below. We were all relieved when Brian traced the source of the water to the air conditioner and stopped the leak.

The slow-motion ride continued into the next day, when we finally reached the Loop Current and turned nearly due south toward Havana. We didn't know it then, but the majority of the fleet that had sailed straight for Cuba was now becalmed. Stopped dead. Just rolling around in the swells. A couple of boats never made it past the Skyway Bridge. Two crews gave up and put in to Key West, where they had a party. Only twenty-two boats finished the race because of the light or nonexistent wind during the first two days. The winner of the race overall was *FOMO*, a forty-footer that ran the course in one day, seventeen hours, zero minutes, and thirty-two seconds.

Despite the torturously slow progress, the ambiance of the open sea captivated me. The vastness, the sheer power, the incredible beauty—it all took hold and captured my imagination. I talked with Brian about it, saying I wanted to get into racing sailboats in a bigger way than I had with the one-designs.

"It's time, Brian. I'm not getting any younger," I said. "Do you know of any good and fast boats for sale?"

The way I see it, life shouldn't be all about work and nothing else. But who am I to talk? My work has been my life for decades, but I've also tried to pay attention to my family. I have two children, a son and a daughter. Nevertheless, I'll be the first to admit that growing and running a prosperous law firm did eat up much of my time. Top attorneys typically work eighty hours a week or more. That's just the way it is. I was born in March 1959, so I was just shy of my fifty-eighth birthday during the race. I'd already begun to feel more inclined to do some of the things I'd put off in my life, and the race brought those feelings to the surface.

"I know of a B-32 that's for sale. I used to own one, and they're excellent racing yachts. The one that's for sale is named *Mad Cow*, if you can believe that," Brian said.

I laughed. "*Mad Cow*? Now there's an interesting name for a boat."

We slowly sailed on. By about midafternoon on the third day, we were all going stir crazy. Dave whipped out his bongo drums and started beating on them, going nuts and having a good old time.

"Hey, can I go fishing?" Dave asked. "Maybe we can catch dinner!"

"Knock yourself out," I said.

I looked over at Brian as Dave and another friend brought out fishing poles and strolled to the stern to fish. Brian just shook his head. This was like no other race he'd ever run. That was for sure, and

I knew it. I doubt he'll ever be in another race like that one again. I doubt I ever will be either.

"Hey, Dave!" I said. "You got some great music down below. Put on some Led Zeppelin, okay?"

He did. We rocked out. Big time.

"Hey, Dave! Why don't we crack open a bottle of champagne? It's blazing hot out here," I said.

Karena, Dave's wife, brought up a nice ice-cold bottle of bubbly, all to the beat of "Stairway to Heaven" and other Zeppelin greatest hits. Time passed. Our GPS told us we were approaching the Gulf Stream, which would set us south and east. I noticed that the wave conditions had changed. The water didn't look all that much different in color, but we were definitely in the Gulf Stream. Even I could see that, and I'd never been offshore before. If you've got a fierce current whipping through otherwise low dark groundswells, it's pretty obvious.

The sun began to set. With no big wind to carry us to Havana, we figured we'd creep into the harbor at some point the next day. We cracked open another bottle of champagne and made the best of the situation.

Cheers!

Suddenly, I felt a puff of wind that was stronger than before. The skin on my neck, wet with sweat, sensed the caress of a rising southwesterly breeze.

"You feel that?" I asked no one in particular.

Then Dave caught a fish, which proceeded to bleed all over the deck. There was much hooting and hollering as we subdued the thrashing and flopping fish. Everything then seemed to happen at once. The breeze filled in quickly. It was perfect for a spinnaker run. Up went the kite, and we were soon speeding toward Havana. The wind built. We went faster. Night fell. The seas kicked up. *Patience* flew downwind. Now *this* was more like it, more of what I'd envisioned when I said I'd do the race. The exhilaration was nothing like what I'd experienced on a one-design. This was something altogether different, and it struck me that the thrill of big-boat racing could become addictive.

Brian and I were the only two crew with any experience with spinnakers. I was on the helm, and Brian was on the spinnaker sheets, trimming and easing as needed to keep the sail full. Most people have seen a boat with a spinnaker up. Most nonsailors don't know that you need a long aluminum pole to hold the sail out from the bow. One end of the pole is attached to the mast, and the other end is attached to the lower outer edge of the sail. There are a bunch of lines that hold the pole up and allow you to adjust the sail as needed.

Spinnaker handling is a learned skill. You have to practice. Indeed, sailing a boat off the wind with or without a chute takes skill. You've got to be quick on the helm. You've got to anticipate what the boat will do before she does it, so you can correct in advance. You almost have to outthink the yacht. In some ways, boats are like horses. You can give the horse its head, but you've got to control where the horse goes.

I knew all of this from my small-boat racing days. What was completely new to me was the experience of sailing fast offshore at night, with a giant chute up and drawing hard. Also, I'd never steered a boat with a wheel before, and it was proving to be quite the challenge as the wind and seas continued to build. With a wheel, you steer like you're driving a car. You turn the wheel in the direction you want the boat to go. One-design boats (and many others, like *Mad Cow*) are steered with a tiller, essentially a stick attached to the rudder. With a tiller, you push the stick one way, and the boat goes the other way. This can get tricky when your muscle memory says push when you need to steer in the other direction if you're on a boat with a wheel.

Add to all this the fact that I was used to sailing with a "Windex," basically a weather vane–like thing mounted on top of the mast that shows you which way the wind is blowing. I was also used to relying on "telltales," light strings tied to the shrouds that provide further visual guidance regarding wind direction. I couldn't see the Windex at *Patience's* masthead, and I couldn't see the telltales. Instead, I had to rely on the apparent-wind indicator at the binnacle. I'd never had to do this before, and it was really difficult for me to process all the constantly changing data. Every second, something changed.

I focused on the instruments, on the helm, and on what Brian was saying as we steered into the darkness. The red and green running lights glowed at the bow. At the stern, we showed a white light. The wind rose to more than twenty knots. I fought the wheel, trying to read the gauges to keep the wind direction constantly right to get the most speed out of the boat. When stronger gusts hit, the boat wanted to head up into the wind, something you don't want when you've got a spinnaker poled out forward. If you get the wind in front of the sail, the sail will back and try to lay the boat down on her beam ends.

I fought the helm and overcompensated, and *Patience* rounded up, beam to the seas. She went way over in a wild broach. We had green water coming over the lee rail. You can get in a lot of trouble if you broach a yacht with her kite up. You can dip the spinnaker pole and break it. You can even lose your mast. To say my heart was in my mouth would be an understatement. The adrenaline rush was amazing. This was nothing like a one-design small-boat race around the buoys. Not even close.

"Jeez, Chip!" Brian said as we got the yacht back on course.

"I'm not used to steering by instruments, at least not like this. We don't have apparent-wind indicators on Flying Scots."

"Steer by the stars," he suggested.

I wasn't used to doing that either.

And then I broached her again. Looking back on it now, I just wasn't good enough to handle those conditions. I'd only sailed small boats, and now we were tearing along at twelve to fourteen knots, about the maximum speed for the boat, in the middle of the night off Cuba.

"I think I better take over," Brian said.

"I think you're right," I said.

We switched places. I manned the sheets. I was better at that. At least I wouldn't put us all in danger again if I broached. At least I wouldn't be the one to kill us if we all went down.

At two or three o'clock in the morning, we knew we were getting close to Havana. The new electronics Dave had purchased for the race were working, but some glitches in the equipment were making it hard to see exactly where we were as we approached the fifty-yard-wide channel leading through a coral reef to the Hemingway International Yacht Club just a bit west of the city. Despite the late hour, there were enough lights ashore to make it tough to judge distance off.

Tension was palpable among all of us as we scanned the rough seas in search of the lights of the first marker at the entrance to the channel. The boat was going like a bat out of hell, the spinnaker drawing hard. We decided to douse the spinnaker, for safety's sake.

"Where are you?" I muttered, lifting my binoculars for another look for the light.

Even with the spinnaker down, the yacht rolled from side to side as she flew down the faces of waves and plowed into the waves ahead, sending sheets of spray flying aft. Suddenly, we spotted the light for the first mark, and it was abeam. We'd almost sailed right past it. I heard breakers on either side of us, but none of us could see them. We didn't have to. If we didn't find and line up with the second marker, we'd be on the reef. If we put keel to coral, we'd all probably die in those winds and seas. We were in a classic lee-shore position, with the wind blowing us toward the land.

"Got it," Brian said.

The important thing is that we found that second marker. We knew where we were. Things didn't calm down until we'd doused the sails, motored into the marina, and tied up at a slip. Once the boat was secure, I just sat there feeling about as wired as I ever had been in my life. I'd learned my lesson. Ocean racing is inherently dangerous. Intellectually, you know it is. But until you've been tested, you won't get a real feel for just how much can quickly go wrong. You also won't get a feel for why we do this. The combination of the adrenaline rush, the camaraderie, and the sheer power of a racing machine out at full tilt on the high seas is nothing like you'll ever experience anywhere else.

> Ocean racing is inherently dangerous. Intellectually, you know it is. But until you've been tested, you won't get a real feel for just how much can quickly go wrong.

The next morning, I looked around at the other boats that had participated in the race. Only the bigger yachts were there. We learned that *Patience* had won her race in her class of boats with similar ratings. At the trophy ceremony, when Dave was presented with the award, you'd have thought he'd just won the America's Cup. I was excited and happy for him. For me, the race was a life-changing event, one that led to many more adventures that would furnish memories to last a lifetime.

2

SERENDIPITY

THE LITTLE SINGLE-PROP PLANE looked like it was in big trouble. It had just taken off from Peter O. Knight Airport near the Davis Island Yacht Club in Tampa, where we were sitting on the porch in preparation for a meeting with the owners of *Mad Cow*, the B-32 Brian had told me about during the Cuba race. The plane's engine sputtered. Clearly, the pilot couldn't gain altitude. The plane swooped in low over the heads of some kids sailing prams right off the yacht club.

Small planes are a common sight around the area because of the tiny airport located in a seaplane basin. The airport once served as a vital transportation hub before the Sunshine Skyway Bridge first opened for business in 1954. Prior to that, you had to drive all the way around Tampa Bay to get from St. Petersburg to Tampa, a time-consuming enterprise if there ever was one. If you had the bucks, you hopped on a plane instead of driving.

"This doesn't look good," I said, nodding toward the plane.

"No, it doesn't," Brian said. "I think somebody should call 911."

Brian looked worried. All of us at the table watched as the plane banked hard and swung around over the bay, losing altitude by the second.

"It's gonna crash, man," one of the people at the table said.

My stomach lurched as the plane hit the water, mercifully clear of any kids and small boats. A huge geyser of spray enveloped the plane. I imagined the terrifying sound of the airplane as it smashed into the bay and tore to pieces. I imagined what was happening inside the cockpit. I felt for the pilot, and I hoped that I wasn't seeing death in real life.

The plane settled into the water and started to sink. Crowds gathered along the shoreline to watch. It was oddly silent, as if everyone collectively knew that life was either on the line or had already been snuffed out. Sirens blared in the distance. The seconds ticked on into minutes. Rescue boats surrounded the sinking plane, and it soon became apparent that the pilot had survived the crash as he was hauled out of the wreckage.

This was not an auspicious beginning to my foray into big-boat sailing as a yacht owner. Yet as in everything in life, stuff happens that you just don't expect. A plane crash before a meeting about *Mad Cow* was simply par for the course in the "unexpected" department.

After the excitement had died down, we met with one of the owners of the boat, Ed Ruark. *Mad Cow* had a reputation in Tampa Bay for consistently winning races in her class. She was something of an institution at the yacht club, and I was anxious to see her. When we finished up with the chitchat, we went to see her on her trailer.

I stood at ground level for a long moment, just staring up at her. She looked fast with her six-foot-plus fin keel. As I climbed the ladder to get topside and stepped aboard, I felt excited about the prospect of owning and racing a boat that was much bigger than a nineteen-foot Flying Scot. One thing that immediately caught my eye was the set of cow horns attached to the bow. *Very interesting,* I thought. *The owners must be really big on the cow theme.*

Below decks, *Mad Cow* had few creature comforts. No wine cellar, no refrigeration, not even a proper head. If you wanted to pee, you'd have to use a bucket. Weight matters on a racing boat. The more weight you add, the slower you're going to go. At thirty-two feet, *Mad Cow* only displaced 4,100 pounds. I figured she'd sail like the wind, and I was right.

I liked the looks of the boat. I thought she'd do just fine for local racing. I knew I didn't know enough to sail her to maximum limits right off the bat, but Brian and the owners said they'd be happy to teach me. We'd just finished the St. Petersburg–Habana race a few days earlier, and I was totally up for making the move into big-boat sailing. I made an offer on *Mad Cow,* and she was mine on a handshake before we officially processed the paperwork. In less than one month, I'd gone from a long hiatus in sailing small one-design racing boats to running an offshore race to Cuba and, just a few days later, to taking the plunge into boat ownership on a larger scale. I joined the St. Petersburg Yacht Club and applied to join the Davis Island Yacht Club. Things were happening fast.

The month of March flew by. Brian, an accomplished sailmaker, made a new suit of sails for *Mad Cow,* and we started racing. I'd been the skipper in literally thousands of small-boat races since I was a kid. I knew how to race. I also knew I didn't know bigger boats. Sailing is the same on principle, no matter how large or small the boat is, but when you move into larger boats the power of the machine changes dramatically. You need winches to handle the loads from the headsails, and you need heavy-duty block and tackle to handle the loads on the mainsail. The forces are exponentially greater on a big boat, and that means you've got to know what you're doing, or you could end up dead.

I knew that I needed help if *Mad Cow* was to stand any chance of winning on the racecourse, and I wasn't afraid to ask for it. One of the keys to success in life and in business is to know what you don't know, and then find and hire people who do know. I'm constantly amazed at how many leaders in business don't really do this. They say they're open-minded about hiring, delegating, and big-picture planning, but their actions instead indicate that they want to control every aspect of the business from the top down. As a consequence, the business doesn't do as well as it should because the talent pool in the company isn't being properly deployed. The success of a business depends on its leadership. A bad leader, just like a bad general, is going to get you into trouble—sometimes trouble you can't get out of.

> The ability to delegate is just as important when you're the skipper as it is when you're a business leader.

A skipper doesn't have to know everything to win, and neither does someone in a leadership position in a business. The trick is to put ego aside and get the job done with the right team, and to use the talents of each team member to achieve a common objective.

The ability to delegate is just as important when you're the skipper as it is when you're a business leader. One crew member might be terrific at sail trim but be a bit slow on sail changes on the foredeck. Another crew member might be a superb tactician, and still another might have a subtle hand at the helm that pays off in light air when every move on a boat matters.

While I may not have been doing much sailing up until the Cuba race, I still hung around with sailors. It wasn't hard to find a good crew for *Mad Cow*. Brian, who had become a good friend, offered to tag along as well. With him aboard, along with his wife, Kat, I knew we'd do well.

In April, the Davis Island Yacht Club held the Tampa Bay Hospice Cup, a race of about fifteen miles featuring yachts in a variety of classes. Of course, we entered *Mad Cow*, and on race day I was ready for a win. I'd never sailed in a staggered start before. With one-designs, you all have the same type of boat, and everyone tries to be the first across the finish line. With a staggered start, the slowest boats take off first, and the fastest boats go last. Theoretically, the fast boats will catch up to the slow boats, so the entire fleet should cross the finish line at about the same time. Of course, it never works out like that, but that's the theory. *Mad Cow* was rated as one of the fastest boats in the fleet. We started about an hour after the first boats had left.

Mad Cow caught some good wind, and we began to close in on the fleet. I stood at the tiller, coaxing every bit of speed I could get out of the boat. The new sails were drawing well, and as the boat heeled to the wind, I felt a sense of freedom and exhilaration that I remembered from the old days when I'd finished first in the fleet in one-design regattas.

We surged past our competitors one by one, gradually closing in on the leaders and finishing a few seconds behind the lead boat. We placed first in our class, which didn't surprise me. *Mad Cow* was anything but a cow.

We racers take our sport seriously, but we also don't mind a big party. After the race, we all relaxed at the yacht club. About halfway through the party, it was time for the awards ceremony. As I walked up to the podium to collect my trophy, I heard a low sound behind me that I swore was a cow mooing. Then more moos.

"Moo! Moo! *Moooo!*"

I still get mooed sometimes when I step up to receive trophies, even though I changed the name of the boat to *Chips All In*. The new name played on my name, carrying on a tradition that began when I bought my powerboat and named her *Chips Ahoy!* I don't get mooed with *Merlin*, but with the former *Mad Cow* ...

I took the trophy, thanked everybody, and left the stage to more moos. All in a day at the races. I was feeling pretty good about the win, and about my new yacht-racing adventures. I was ready to do more.

I'd been snooping around the yacht-charter market to see what it would cost to rent a racing boat large enough to brave the potential monster seas and screaming winds on the 635-mile race from Newport, Rhode Island, to Bermuda. My dad had run the race twice in the mid-1950s. He'd always spoken excitedly about the adventure whenever it came up in conversation. I was determined to take him on the 2018 Bermuda race. But I wanted to do it on just the right boat.

"You know," Donice, my girlfriend, said during one of our many discussions about the possibility of doing the Bermuda race, "your parents aren't getting any younger. You only have so much more time when Bill is going to be able to do the race. You should go for it, Chip!"

I intended to do just that. The problem was that I didn't like my options. Charter costs ranged anywhere from $40,000 to $400,000. A charter is essentially a rental, and for four hundred grand I thought it would make sense to just buy a boat. As time dragged on, my frustration grew. It was all about finding a boat that called to me, one that felt right, one that just seemed to say, "Here I am! Come get me!"

In July, the yachting press focused on the latest running of the Transpacific Yacht Race. I'd long known about the Transpac, and the history of the race fascinated me. It all began back in 1886, when Hawaii's King David Kalakaua proposed a yacht race from California to Hawaii as a way of promoting ties between Hawaii and the United

States. Hawaii was a sovereign nation before we annexed it in 1898 during the aftermath of the Spanish-American War. In 1900, Hawaii became an official territory of the United States, achieving statehood only in August 1959. King Kalakaua's great idea didn't catch on until Honolulu businessman Clarence W. Macfarlane revived the notion of a transpacific yacht race in 1906.

Macfarlane sailed his forty-eight-foot schooner, *La Paloma*, to San Francisco with the hope of drumming up interest in the race among the city's elite yachtsmen. When he arrived, he found the city in ruins after the earthquake of 1906. Widespread fires had leveled entire neighborhoods. Obviously, the elite of San Francisco had more on their minds than a yacht race, so Macfarlane sailed down to Los Angeles to have a chat with Harry Sinclair, the commodore of the South Coast Yacht Club and owner of the sleek and fast eighty-six-foot schooner *Lurline*.

A chum of Sinclair's, Charles Tutt, just happened to be visiting from New York City. Macfarlane and Sinclair discussed the idea of the race, and Tutt, owner of the 112-foot ketch *Anemone*, was all in.

The first Transpac race kicked off on June 11, 1906, with the three yachts racing on a handicap system. The handicap system gave a time allowance to smaller yachts racing against larger yachts. The big boat *Lurline* won the roughly 2,225-nautical-mile race with an elapsed time of twelve days and ten hours.

Over time, the race evolved. For example, it used to be run on even-numbered years, which put it in competition with the Newport-Bermuda race. Nowadays, the Transpac runs on odd-numbered years, drawing sailors and yachts from around the globe. The race features a variety of yacht classes, from traditional sloops to space-age catamarans. Today the start is staggered, so the slower and faster fleets arrive off Diamond Head, Oahu, at about the same time. In theory, anyway.

During the two world wars, the race went on hiatus, and the event almost fizzled out during the Great Depression. In 1932, only two entries registered for the race. But interest in the race continued. In 1934, twelve boats started. The 1930s marked the first signs of a decline in gaff-rigged schooners (gaffs are wooden spars on which the top edge of a sail is mounted). Based on the working yachts of the 1800s, vessels of this venerable design resemble old-fashioned ships in a bottle and had dominated the race from the start.

Modern yacht design was making inroads with modified fin keels, less "wetted" surfaces, and highly efficient rigs that could drive a sloop, ketch, or yawl fast and hard on the downwind ride to Hawaii. As opposed to gaffs, the modern yachts sported Bermuda (also known as Marconi) rigs that featured more aerodynamically efficient triangular sails, with only the bottom edge mounted to a spar (boom). Gaff rigs are unheard of today in production yachts (as opposed to custom-made yachts), though you can still see plenty of them up in Maine's fleet of historic schooners.

Nine decades later, the Transpac had become one of the premiere events for ocean racers. As a new member of the ocean racing club, I was paying attention. Of particular interest were stories about a boat I'd first read about in 1978, the iconic yacht *Merlin*. Her original owner, yacht builder and designer Bill Lee, had bought her from her latest owner, Jere Sullivan, in the Midwest, trucked the boat to Santa Cruz, California, and proceeded to outfit her for the 2017 Transpac.

Bill Lee had designed and built *Merlin* specifically to win the Transpac in 1977. He succeeded by setting an elapsed-time course record of eight days, eleven hours, one minute, and forty-five seconds to cover the passage of more than two thousand nautical miles. That record stood for twenty years, which is impressive because innovations in racing yacht designs continued to make great strides subsequent to the race. The boats got lighter and lighter, in large part due to Bill's successful designs. When something's good, it gets copied.

The sailing press was all over the story, especially since two new records were set in the 2017 Transpac. The one-hundred-foot sloop *Comanche* set an astonishing monohull record of five days, one hour, fifty-five minutes, and twenty-six seconds. *Merlin*'s 2017 elapsed time was eight days, two hours, thirty-four minutes, and nine seconds, beating her 1977 record by more than nine hours. *Mighty Merloe*, an ORMA 60 trimaran (three hulls), set the multihull record with a run of four days, six hours, thirty-two minutes, and thirty seconds. *Rio*, a ninety-nine-foot Bakewell-White sloop built in 2003, won the Barn Door Trophy, given to the first yacht to cross the finish line. Her elapsed time was six days, seventeen hours, nine minutes, and nine seconds. She also won the Barn Door in the 2015 Transpac. She's a mighty impressive yacht!

The Barn Door Trophy is so named because it's big, at three and a half feet by four feet. The trophy is made of hand-carved Hawaiian koa wood, and it proudly says, "First to Finish." The Barn Door rules have undergone a few changes since the early days of the race, but the trophy still is one of the most sought after.

As I read about *Merlin*'s exploits in 2017, I thought about that *Sports Illustrated* article from 1978. Back then, I was nineteen and slaving away as an undergraduate majoring in business administration at the University of Florida. Sitting on one of the ratty couches in my frat house, I'd thumbed through a copy of the magazine. I stopped dead when I opened the spread that showed *Merlin* under sail during the Transpac.

Obviously, the yacht's name intrigued me, because Merlin is my last name. Still, the sheer speed of the boat jumped off the page. From the trail of broken water in her wake to the white froth at her bow, she surged like a greyhound with a prodigious bone in her teeth.

Wow! I thought. *What a boat! I'm gonna buy that boat if I ever have the means and the opportunity!*

Fast-forward to a night in October of 2017 when I was poking around the internet on my iPad looking for that elusive boat for the Bermuda race. Then I saw the ad. My eyes widened. My heart rate increased. I took a deep breath and said to Donice, "My God! *Merlin*'s for sale!"

Donice smiled, shook her head. "That boat's gonna get bought," she said.

I knew she was right. I wanted that boat. *I really wanted that boat!*

Things happened fast. I called Bill right then, left a message, and tried to get some sleep. He called me back the next day, and I explained who I was.

Nobody knew me in big-boat racing circles, but having a reputation in racing can be important if you're buying an iconic yacht like *Merlin*. Some owners can be very picky about who they sell their boats to. I told Bill I could have my captain, Brian, fly out to Santa Cruz, and I could get there the following day, after I took an important deposition in New York City.

That's exactly what we did.

I flew straight from New York to San Jose, grabbed an Uber at the airport, and headed to my hotel to catch up with Brian, who had already met with Bill and checked out the boat. In the car, I could see and smell smoke from all the wildfires burning at the time. As an attorney specializing in representing property owners in disputes with their insurance companies, I knew there would be a lot of cases for the firm. I felt sad for the people who were losing their homes, and I knew that many of those victims would probably need an advocate to help them get the money they deserved from the insurance companies.

At the same time, my mind was on *Merlin*. The chance to buy her almost didn't seem real. I'd fallen for the boat nearly forty years earlier. It seemed incredible that she could actually be mine.

The following morning, we drove to Santa Cruz Marina to meet Bill and go for a sail. Coming down the dock, I could see the blue hull of a long and skinny boat. I was astonished at how big she was compared to *Mad Cow*, a.k.a. *Chips All In*. Although I knew she was seventy-one feet in overall length, I wasn't prepared for the scale. Next to her, *Mad Cow* looked like a dinghy. The winches were mammoth. The spinnaker pole looked long enough to use as a spare mast.

In the slip next to her was a Santa Cruz 70. I'd been under the mistaken impression that *Merlin* was just like one of these fast ultra-light displacement boats that had shaken up West Coast sailing. After all, Bill Lee had designed and built a whole pack of Santa Cruz racers. Many are still winning races and setting records. *Merlin* didn't resemble them. She looked smaller and sleeker.

Boy, you're way out of your league, I thought as I talked with Bill and the friends he'd brought along to help sail *Merlin*. *You've gotta be outa your freakin' mind!* But even as I thought it, I felt differently.

There are always naysayers. Some people said I was nuts to start my own law firm at the ripe age of twenty-six. The big thing is not to listen to people who tell you that you can't do something, that you're dumb to take risks, and that you should toe the conventional line. I try to be guided by my own inner compass. I tend to trust those gut feelings about whether a given action is right or wrong. If I don't know something, I ask an expert to fill me in. A good leader puts ego aside at all times and is never afraid to rely on the expertise of others in the pursuit of a team's mission.

As I craned my neck to look up at the wind vane perched on the very top of the mast, it just felt right to be aboard the boat.

"Shall we take her out?" Bill asked. "We've got light wind, but I know where to find the pockets … enough to get her going. Doesn't take much, really."

Brian and I jumped right in with the rest of the crew as Bill fired up the motor and we cast off the lines, took in the fenders, and got the sail cover off the main. Under power, she barely disturbed the water. Santa Cruz Harbor is small, just a gash in the coast. As we nosed out the inlet, the rock breakwaters on either side, I was amazed at the number of seals sunning themselves and barking at each other. We don't have seals on the Gulf Coast, so seeing them was a reminder of when I lived in Monterey for a year as a kid. A slight haze shrouded the shoreline. Part of it was smoke from the wildfires, and part of it was due to fog generated by the temperature differential between the warm land and the cold Pacific. I'd never sailed on the Pacific before. It was another first among any number of firsts in that eventful year.

The swells rolled lazily in toward shore as we got out into the ocean, the bow lifting and falling in a gentle rhythm. We hoisted the sails, which flogged with thunderous bangs until Bill eased her off the wind and killed the engine. The sails were massive, like nothing I'd ever experienced. With the main and the jib, she carried an astounding 1,834 square feet of sail. I felt the yacht accelerate, despite the light winds. I watched the knot meter climb steadily … five, six, seven, eight knots. I looked at the wind-speed indicator, and I was shocked to see that the boat was sailing faster than the wind.

What kind of boat is this? I wondered.

Bill offered me the helm. I definitely didn't want to look like I didn't know what I was doing, even though I definitely didn't. As we picked up speed, I noticed she was very light on the helm. I would have thought that the steering action on such a big boat would be heavy, but to my immense amazement she steered like a dinghy.

We got on a downwind heading, and up went the spinnaker, with me still on the helm. *Merlin* immediately picked up more speed, as if I'd just hit the gas on a Lamborghini.

"Head her up a little more," Bill said.

I turned the wheel ever so slightly (I could steer with the index finger of my right hand) and brought the wind closer to the bow, hoping and praying I wouldn't backwind the spinnaker. *Merlin* sped up. She left an arrow-straight wake behind her that looked like a motorboat's. I'd heard that the yacht could actually get up on plane and surf down those big Pacific swells with her stern squat in the water and the bow up. I think Bill wanted to get her to do that, but the wind wasn't quite strong enough. Despite the relatively light air, we hit about fifteen knots with the kite up.

"This is amazing," I said. "*Amazing!*"

I think Bill knew he'd made a sale, probably from the moment I first talked to him and told him my last name was Merlin. The deal was done, at least in my mind. I knew from then on out that nothing would ever be the same for me again. I was about to enter an elite world of big-boat ocean racing with a dream boat, and there was no turning back.

3

DREAMS

WE'VE ALL HEARD the saying, "Oh, he's just a dreamer." And there are people like that, people with zero pragmatism or practicality. Maybe they choose to live in a fantasy world of their own making, or maybe they sit glued to their screens watching reality television contests, or playing video games. It's a valid choice, though I think it can keep us from living our lives with the greatest potential for happiness and success. It's too easy to get trapped in the cycle of admiring and envying celebrities or wishing away our time.

While I don't believe in dreaming the *impossible* dream (some dreams are truly impossible, such as becoming an NFL star at age fifty), I do think that having a purpose in life is one of the keys to happiness and success, both on a personal and professional level. I've long thought that the pursuit of something important to us as unique individuals is vital to leading a fulfilling existence. Without purpose, there can be no happiness. We just drift aimlessly along like autumn leaves on a river, the current taking us wherever it wants to go, as opposed to our taking active steps to steer our lives in the direction we want to go.

I think most of us dream in some way or another, and that doesn't make us dreamers in the negative sense. Indeed, our dreams make us who we are, and who we will be. The trick is to set a goal. You often hear people joke about doing something they love in another life. "Oh, I'll get around to it someday," they say, but they never do. They've bought into their own excuse for not taking action to pursue their dreams.

For many of us, it's safer to do nothing to move toward our dreams. Daily routines swallow us whole. We barely have time to think, much less dream. Routine is predictable and comfortable. I would contend that inertia comes from a fear of the unknown and, for some of us, from an innate laziness that sets us up for failure. Fear of failure itself stops some of us in our tracks. Don't get me wrong: I love to win. But I'm not afraid to fail either. We can and should learn from our mistakes and setbacks.

There's a saying in Maine about people who don't seem to use their boats much, and it's a commentary on life in general: "If you haven't hit a rock, you haven't left the dock." How true! If we don't set sail into the unknown, if we haven't hit that proverbial rock, we haven't exposed ourselves to the risks and rewards that come from putting ourselves out there in the world to see what will happen next.

Bill Lee exemplifies this idea. He put himself out there, and great things happened. But it didn't all just happen at once. The evolution of Bill Lee as a yacht designer and builder took time. It was a hard journey to the top, as it always is. As the expression goes, "Anything worth doing takes effort."

To dream big requires you to like doing the tough stuff to get where you want to go. If being a success were easy, then everyone would rise to the pinnacle of their chosen professions. Of course, not everyone can stand at the podium. I think it's important to know that even when you've tried as hard as you can and you don't rise to the top, it doesn't mean you've failed. The real failure lies in not trying at all. That's as true on the racecourse as it is in the company boardroom.

Born in Coeur d'Alene, Idaho, Bill Lee didn't start sailing until his family moved to Newport Beach, California, when he was fifteen. He raced El Toro dinghies, joined the Sea Scouts, and crewed for owners of large ocean racing yachts while he was in high school. After Bill graduated from Cal Poly at San Luis Obispo in 1965 with a degree in mechanical engineering, he went to work in the defense industry in Southern California.

The Vietnam conflict was heating up at the time, and we would soon be embroiled in an all-out shooting war with the Vietcong and the North Vietnamese. Part of Bill's work included detailed analyses of stress, weight, trim, and other factors as a member of a design team developing the prototype of a new armored personnel carrier. It was a rather establishment sort of job. He wasn't happy working for the war machine. He'd envisioned a different life, but he wasn't sure exactly what that life would entail. He wasn't passionate about designing personnel carriers. But he was passionate about boats.

In 1969, on his twenty-sixth birthday, he quit his job and moved to Santa Cruz, with tentative plans to go sailing with friends for a year while he figured out what he wanted to do with his life. It didn't take him long to start putting his design skills and passion for sailing to work.

Fiberglass has been around since the early 1930s. Glass wool was invented by the engineer Russell Games Slayter for thermal insulation in construction. In 1936, Carlton Ellis of DuPont earned the patent for polymer resin. Resin met glass wool shortly thereafter, giving us a world of fiberglass objects from boats to aircraft to auto parts and beyond. Fiberglass boats came into vogue in the late 1950s, displacing wood as the most common boatbuilding material. Fiberglass was still relatively new when Bill established Bill Lee Yachts in the early 1970s, first starting with custom builds and then moving into production boats.

Early fiberglass boats were way overbuilt. Builders used heavy fiberglass cloth and a great deal of resin in the belief that stronger was safer at sea. But it was heavy, and heavy is slow. Bill liked to sail fast. The logo for Bill Lee Yachts sums it up: "Fast is fun." Bill instinctively knew that weight translated to slow, and he was convinced that light would translate into fast.

The challenge was to finesse the right design, which he did for a radical thirty-foot racing sloop he named *Magic*. Using the 505 dinghy as inspiration, Bill's plan was to make a light and strong sloop from fiberglass using a balsa core sandwiched between thin layers of fiberglass. The technology wasn't new. Core hulls had been made before, either with balsa or foam. Bill thought balsa would be stronger, so he went with that instead of foam.

Working odd jobs, he saved up enough money to begin work on the boat in an outdoor lot. When he needed help, he threw keg parties for all his friends, who were more than willing to pitch in for a few cold brews. It took about a year to finish the boat because work stopped when Bill ran out of money and had to find another odd job to pay for his boatbuilding habit. In the spring of 1970 *Magic* was launched, with plenty of beer and good cheer. Bill wore a magician's cape (some say it was a wizard's hat) to play off the boat's name.

Magic was amazingly light, displacing just 2,500 pounds and carrying nearly 450 square feet of sail. In short, she was lighter than most boats her size, and she carried much more sail than a typical thirty-footer. It's worth noting that very few yacht designers also build boats. Designers and builders usually stay in two separate camps. Bill admits that the build wasn't as professional as it could have been. Yet he worked with what he had to transform *Magic* from a dream into a reality.

I've always believed that you have to do something, whatever it is, over and over again before you can be the best. I'm a much better attorney now than when I first got into the law. That's the natural way of things. We get better with experience. So did Bill.

Bill was just starting out, but what an auspicious beginning. *Magic* won the Monterey Bay series and the Monterey–Santa Barbara race. Bill and his boat soon attracted a lot of attention from racing enthusiasts because *Magic* was so fast, and because she was so light.

She represented something new, something different, and the West Coast racing community noticed. *Magic* threatened the norm. She was so radical that the overbuilt racers she was sailing against were at a distinct disadvantage when sailing downwind. Upwind, the heavier boats fared better, but Bill didn't care much about thrashing to windward with spray flying aft over the bow. He wanted to set the spinnaker and sail like a witch, as they say in New England.

The following year, one *Magic* fan, a man by the name of Art Biehi, asked Bill if he'd like to crew on the Transpacific Yacht Race. Art had been inched out of wins in previous Transpacs, and he didn't win honors again in that year's race. Biehi wanted a boat that would win the Transpac, and he figured Bill would be a good guy to talk to about a custom build. Bill said he'd be happy to oblige. The result was *Witchcraft*, a thirty-five-foot sloop that displaced just 7,500 pounds and carried 600 square feet of sail. The forty-foot *Panache*, which Bill built for himself, was beamy and fast. The thirty-six-foot *Chutzpa*, a sister ship to *Panache*, followed. All the boats did exceptionally well on the racecourse, and Bill was on his way.

Chutzpa won overall corrected honors in the 1973 and 1975 Transpac. When *Chutzpa* won the first time, there was a big party (as usual). Bill wore a pointy wizard hat made by a friend at a local sail loft, in part because Bill's "magic" theme caught on as his boats gained acclaim in racing circles. After that memorable party, people started calling Bill "the Wizard."

As with all legends, the story gets mixed up in the retelling. When did the wizard hat really show up? It's hard to tell, but the wizard theme was well executed at the party after the finish of the 1977 Transpac, with Bill grinning ear to ear in his wizard's costume.

Most every small start-up begins on a shoestring budget. Bill's business was no exception. He decided to move into production boat-building in addition to custom builds to get his business off the ground in a bigger way. A production fiberglass boat is built in a mold. With a mold, you turn out the same hull and deck structures time after time, like cookies from a cookie cutter.

Bill dreamed up a design for a fast twenty-seven-footer, the Santa Cruz 27, that seemed like an ideal choice for production. After searching for a suitable location to establish a small boatbuilding facility, he discovered that the buildings were a bit pricey in Santa Cruz. Even in the early 1970s. The property he could afford was a defunct egg-laying facility. The lot included a 10,000-square-foot concrete slab and a narrow 200-foot-long chicken coop. It was located about four miles south of Santa Cruz on a hill, so access to the bay would require a flatbed truck. As with everything in life and in business, there's usually a workaround to a problem, and Bill found his with a giant chicken coop.

Up went a small sign nailed to a telephone pole at the entry road that said, "Bill Lee Yachts." The parking lot sat about thirty feet below the coop. You climbed old wooden stairs to get to the door. A sign on the door read, "Bring a six-pack."

Plenty of six-packs showed up under the arms of would-be owners of Bill Lee boats. The Santa Cruz 27 went into production in 1974. Displacing 3,000 pounds, she adhered to the class design of boats popular at the time, the quarter tonners. The price was within reach of many sailors, at just $17,000. The Santa Cruz 27 was one of the more popular models from Bill Lee Yachts. Something like 145 Santa Cruz 27s were built in the next decades. And while no new ones have come off the production line recently, the Santa Cruz 27 National Championship is still held annually.

A year or so later, Bill entered *Panache* in the 1,100-mile San Diego–Manzanillo race to Mexico. After the race, he and his crew were partying with the crew of *Ragtime*, a Spencer 53 with a narrow beam and hard chines. She'd won line honors in the Transpac earlier in the year. Bill liked her design, but he saw some potential in it for additional development. He was also toying with the idea of running in the 1977 Transpac. Like his customers, he wanted a boat that would win.

Carrying the ultralight concept to the extreme, Bill hit the drafting table and designed *Merlin*, which would become the prototype of the venerable Santa Cruz 70 (Bill went on to build nineteen of them). As he scoped out the specs, he realized that the chicken coop was going to factor into the design. In order to fit the yacht inside his building, the beam of the boat would have to be rather narrow. The coop was long and skinny, just the way *Merlin* turned out.

It's always interested me to see how circumstances can chart new paths as you work around setbacks and obstacles in life and business. Bill didn't have room to make a beamy boat, and he didn't want to anyway. *Ragtime* was on his mind. He figured narrow would be fast, and he was certainly correct.

Like many iconic racing yachts, *Merlin* has gone through extensive modifications over the years. I commissioned some myself in preparation for the 2019 Transpac. When the boat was first launched, she was 66.5 feet in overall length. In the 1980s, a stern scoop was added, nudging her overall length up to sixty-eight feet. A stubby bowsprit brought her up to her current seventy-one feet in overall length. She originally displaced 24,000 pounds, sporting a skinny fin keel with a draft of nine feet and 10,500 pounds of ballast. She now draws close to eleven feet with her latest keel.

Bill chose balsa-core construction with E-glass and woven roving. Bill's training in the defense industry came in handy as he whittled the build down to the limits of structural integrity without compromising safety at sea. The interior structures of the boat were built from Bruynzeel plywood. The accommodations were beyond spartan. The layout included ten berths, a raised settee over the water tanks, a navigation station, a galley, and a tiny head crammed forward in the bow.

Bill and his team were determined to win the Transpac in *Merlin*. They all pitched in to make it happen. Four guys worked for about ten months on the build. When extra help was needed, Bill bought a keg and threw a *Merlin*-building party. Nobody had seen anything like the yacht. At her launch in February 1977, Bill was pretty much out of cash. He told me that he'd sunk 80 percent of his net worth into the yacht by the time he was ready to splash her.

"I should've had my head examined," he said with a laugh as we talked about those crazy times.

The first sail revealed just how fast Bill's design was. Downwind, with the mainsail alone, the speedo was registering twelve knots before they set the mammoth spinnaker for the first time. The kite went up, the helmsman bore off to fill the sail, and *Merlin* took off like a rocket, surging to seventeen knots in a matter of about twenty seconds.

Some who were on the first sail said it was like riding a motorboat without the engine. The description is apt. When *Merlin* is rocking out downwind, it looks like she's shooting up a rooster tail from a secret jet engine hidden below the waterline.

Further sea trials confirmed that *Merlin* was unique, and even a little scary. When she got up on plane as she surfed the backs of big Pacific swells, she hit well over twenty knots. One crew member recalled being on the foredeck during a sail change when the boat surfed down a wave and speared through the next one, dipping the foredeck under three feet of green water. The force of the water lifted the sailor up, washed him down the foredeck, and dumped him into the open forehatch. He hung upside down in his safety harness as the Pacific flowed into the boat. He called the experience the "cosmic flush."

The crew soon got used to cosmic flushes. They happened all the time. What struck nearly everyone as unusual was that the yacht didn't slow down or load up. She simply slid through the waves as if it was completely normal for a 66.5-foot yacht to perform like a submarine. The crew admitted that it was terrifying the first time they experienced a *Das Boot* moment, but they soon got used to it as they continued to shake *Merlin* down in coastal races off San Francisco prior to the Transpac.

Word got out about how the boat handled at sea. Crew members said she was extremely lively, meaning she would heel easily and pitch in a seaway. She required constant sail changes to keep her moving at maximum speed. I can say from experience that *Merlin* is not a comfortable boat to sail on. Everything happens fast, and you frequently have to hold on to something just to move around above or below deck. *Merlin's* motion grows really nasty in choppy conditions, especially sailing to windward. If you suffer from mal de mer, *Merlin* will nudge you to the edge.

> There are always tradeoffs in life, business, and boats.

There are always tradeoffs in life, business, and boats. In Bill's case, he designed her for one thing: winning the Transpac. Critics of the design said she was unsafe. I think they were simply unaware of the virtues of Bill's design. Designed for downwind sailing, she didn't need to be heavily built. Traditional racing yachts at the time were much heavier, as I've said, and these boats could sail well to windward, but they'd pound in rough seas and strong winds when sailing close-hauled. In short, the heavy boats took a beating when the weather got up, whereas *Merlin* tended to act like a Ping-Pong ball, giving way to the forces of the wind and sea instead of fighting them.

Bill paid little attention to the growing crowd of naysayers who claimed the boat was a deathtrap and that she'd ruin the Transpac because the traditional boats wouldn't stand a chance against her on a downwind run. It wasn't fair, they said. As boat design changed generally, changes in the rules eventually caught up, but there was a hue and cry about fairness at the time.

The bulk of the Transpac is run in the northeasterly trade winds. With the wind off the stern, the fleet flies. At the start of the race, the fleet must beat upwind past the Santa Barbara Islands, and then head along the southeast edge of the Pacific High. From there, it's all downhill sailing in long Pacific swells, with tropical breezes and puffy fair-weather cumulus clouds sprinkled across a brilliant blue sky, all the way to Molokai Channel and the finish at Diamond Head.

On race day 1977, five boats in the fleet were cast as favorites to win overall. The two traditional heavier-displacement boats were

Windward Passage and *Kialoa III*. *Merlin* was racing against two other formidable ultralightweight displacement yachts, *Drifter* and *Ragtime*.

Merlin surged out in front of the majority of the fleet, surfing and submarining all the way, but *Drifter* led her for six of the eight days before the finish. The two yachts jockeyed for the lead, with *Merlin* pulling ahead in the last two days. On that run, she logged passages of more than three hundred nautical miles per twenty-four hours. Just to put that in perspective, that kind of a run would have been viewed as exceptional on a clipper ship. On the final day, *Merlin* still held the lead. *Drifter* was hot on her tail, and the race still hung in the balance. If *Merlin*'s crew made a mistake, the race would most likely be lost.

The wind piped up at about twenty knots. Skies were overcast. Huge ocean swells rolled into Molokai Channel as *Merlin* and *Drifter* headed toward the finish at Diamond Head with spinnakers flying and drawing fair. One more jibe and *Merlin* would be lined up for the final blast. Bill ordered the kite dropped before the jibe, intending to run a second chute up as soon as the jibe was complete. About five miles back, *Drifter*'s crew jibed with the chute up. The boat broached, crashing beam to the swells so far over her that the spreaders hit the water. She could have been dismasted.

Suddenly, a C-135 flew overhead and circled to give the photographer good angles to shoot. *Merlin* flew off the top of a big swell, and down the bow went in yet another submarine event. The photographer got the dive on film, and people were amazed when the photo was published. The plane turned and headed out to shoot *Drifter*. *Merlin* surged on, crossing the finish line seventeen minutes ahead of *Drifter* and setting a speed record that would not be broken for two decades. The crew was ecstatic, and none was happier than Bill. The Wizard had struck again.

For Bill, winning the Transpac in 1977 marked a milestone moment in his life. With *Merlin* as inspiration for the venerable Santa Cruz 70, she'd also set the trend in racing yacht design. Just about every racing boat you see these days is built on the ultra-light-displacement model.

In some ways, Bill's early career matched mine. We both figured we had a life plan, and then change came, as it inevitably does. Bill found himself jumping from the defense industry to yacht design and boatbuilding. I found myself changing plans in August 1977, just before I matriculated at the University of Florida. At the time, I thought I'd study business administration, and then go on to pursue my MBA. I've always loved math, finance, and business. Pursuing a life in the corporate world seemed like a good idea.

Then it happened.

Some friends and I were on our way to go bluefishing on Chesapeake Bay when another vehicle ran a stop sign and T-boned the station wagon we were in. The impact pushed us into the oncoming lane, where we slammed head-on into a VW microbus. I was sitting in the back seat. Glass shattered. Metal tore and screamed as the car practically disintegrated. Blood covered everything.

Instead of bluefishing, my friends and I ended up in the hospital for four days.

My elbow was dislocated, and my thumb was broken. Decades later, I still can't straighten my arm all the way.

The accident was clearly the fault of the other driver. I thought it was a little odd that Dad chose to settle without an attorney. Years later I discovered that my grandfather had had some bad experiences with commercial lawyers in Tampa, so attorneys weren't exactly on my dad's Christmas card list.

What's that line? "It's easy to hate lawyers—until you need them."

That traumatic event showed me just how life can come bite you when you least expect it. One minute everything's fine, and the next minute it isn't. You get into a car accident, your house or business burns down, or a storm destroys or wrecks your property. What are you going to do if you don't know your rights and can't negotiate with the insurance company from a position of authority and knowledge? I didn't know my rights at the time, which bothered me. My friends and I were at the mercy of the insurance company to pay a fair settlement.

I began to consider a career in the law with a focus on litigation, and by the end of the first fall semester at the University of Florida, I'd decided to dedicate my life to the law. That accident changed my life, just as Bill quitting the defense industry changed his.

I've come a long way since my days in college, and I've come a long way since I took my first sail with my dad on a Sailfish at age five. I credit him with fostering my love of sailing, a love that has resurfaced in my life since that eventful 2017 Cuba race with Dave Kilcoyne aboard the intrepid *Patience*. It's interesting how dreams grow and evolve, if you let them, and if you work hard at pursuing them. As I've said, we all have our dreams. The dreams taking shape in 2017 all began with my dad.

Dad served in the coast guard, which meant we moved constantly whenever he received orders to a new duty station. When I was eleven years old, we moved to Waveland, Mississippi, with a population of about five thousand. My mom wasn't too happy about the move because Mississippi had a reputation as being backward and a poor place to live in terms of educating kids. As it turned out, the three years I spent in Mississippi were some of the happiest of my youth. I attended Saint Stanislaus, a private boys school run by the Brothers of the Sacred Heart. They challenged me to push to the limits. I learned how satisfying hard work can be if you're passionate about what you're doing.

Almost immediately upon our arrival, Dad joined the Bay Waveland Yacht Club, which sailed out of the Bay of Saint Louis, Mississippi. The club had an active junior sailing program, and I threw myself into it, racing Flying Scots six days a week during the summer. I learned how to sail competitively, and about the importance of teamwork when pitching in on a common effort. Sailing didn't come naturally to me. I had to work at it. You never start as the skipper. You never start out as the CEO either. Learning the ropes on Flying Scots taught me that to be good at something takes practice and experience. That's a lesson that paid off when I went to law school, passed the Florida bar, and got my first job in a Tampa-based law firm in early 1983.

> Learning the ropes on Flying Scots taught me that to be good at something takes practice and experience.

When I started Merlin Law Group in 1985 with the express purpose of helping policyholders get a fair deal from insurance companies, some people said I would fail. They told me I was too young to sally forth on my own at the age of twenty-six to practice law. It would have been much safer for me to stay with an established law firm, but I knew what I wanted to do. I left the dock, hitting more than a few of those proverbial rocks along the way, and I never looked back. Ironically, taking the risks I did and working as hard as I did were what allowed me to follow through on my dream of buying *Merlin*, and on taking my dad on the 2018 Newport-Bermuda race.

4

TEAMWORK

MY MIND WOULD NOT stop working overtime as I stared out the window of the plane at the broad expanse of sky as I flew home from Santa Cruz. In many ways, buying Merlin and putting together a yacht-racing team marked a plunge into the unknown for me. While I always welcome a new challenge and encourage change when it's positive, I found myself almost feeling nervous about the adventure I had embarked on, practically on a whim.

One minute I'd been looking to charter a suitable boat to race to Bermuda with my dad, and in the next minute I was the proud owner of an iconic seventy-one-foot racing yacht that I didn't even really know how to sail. As the hours passed and the plane continued droning east, I went over the basics of the action plan I'd come up with. Much needed to be done to get the boat ready for the 2018 St. Petersburg–Habana race, which was slated for February 26. It would be a trial run for the race to Bermuda.

But we first had to get *Merlin* from Santa Cruz to the East Coast on an oversize flatbed truck that barely fit the one-hundred-foot maximum length. Propped upright with jack stands and lashed down tight, she stood tall in the bed of that truck. In fact, she would just fit under overpasses.

Typically, you'd sail a racer like *Merlin* to the next port, but moving her from the West Coast to the East Coast of the United States would have meant a passage of many thousands of miles via the Panama Canal. A lot of bad things can happen to a boat (and her crew) when sailing offshore for extended periods. Avoiding the voyage's wear and tear on the boat made trucking her more sensible. In addition, trucking the boat the 2,900 miles from California to Florida was actually less expensive than sailing her, and of course, it was much faster as well. We also had to figure out where we could find a slip for a seventy-one-foot boat—a feat easier said than done, but we managed.

I'd need to have the boat thoroughly checked over before pointing her bow offshore, even for the relatively short jaunt south to Havana. And there was a team to assemble, and gear to gather, and a zillion details I could barely anticipate, like refinishing the hull, optimizing the rig, upgrading the sails, and doing what we could to make a fast boat even faster.

Obviously, I needed help.

From long experience, I can say that the best leaders know their limitations and that they surround themselves with people armed with the knowledge needed to get the job done right. For example, some attorneys in my law firm are better litigators than I am. Don't get me wrong. I am a heck of a good trial lawyer, but in some instances another member of my legal team will be a better match for a particular client and case. It simply makes sense to use the skills of the people around you, and to constantly work with the team to improve the skill sets of everyone from the receptionist to the CEO. Continuous training and education are a requirement in most professions. The law is no exception. The same goes for sailboat racing. You never stop learning.

I needed a good team. Enter Brian Malone.

Brian Malone had been sailing for most of his life. A native of Hopetown, Bahamas, he ran a fishing boat in the Bahamas for many years. He then worked as a sailmaker and rigger in St. Petersburg, Florida. He'd been more than willing to help me with *Mad Cow*, a.k.a. *Chips All In*, and he agreed to help me with *Merlin* by managing the yacht and recruiting professional sailors to make the boat as successful as possible on the racecourse. Brian knew top players in ocean yacht-racing circles, and I figured that with him at the helm, putting a crew together would be no problem.

I also met with the chief operating officer of Merlin Law Group, Keona Williams, early on in the purchase process to share my vision of how the boat would factor into the law practice. I wanted to make it clear that I wasn't buying the boat to ease off work and go sailing. Far from it.

Not only would the boat help promote the law firm, but I also hoped it would provide interesting material for the motivational speeches I give to business leaders all over the country. Coordinating the details on *Merlin* would be up to her and Brian. I'd stick with what I was good at, the law, and let the experts handle the yacht.

After I returned to Tampa, word got out fast that I was *Merlin's* new owner. Almost immediately, sailors from all over the United States were sending me their sailing résumés and asking to join the team. What did I know about sailing résumés? Absolutely nothing.

If you know what you don't know and you admit it, you're already

If you know what you don't know and you admit it, you're already ahead of the game.

ahead of the game. The logical next step is to find someone with the expertise to fill the knowledge gap, and then empower that individual to move forward with the job at hand in the way he or she sees fit. We've all witnessed the tendency among some leaders to micromanage, to resist giving up control, and to lack the flexibility to respond nimbly to the market forces that will inevitably exert pressure on the company. Ego rules. And sound decision-making goes right out the window.

I didn't want that to happen with Team *Merlin*. I wanted the crew to buy into my vision for the boat, and it had to start with Brian as the team leader.

The practice of empowering people, emboldening them, and letting them know that they have the power and flexibility to do their jobs in the best way possible leads to effective teamwork, whereas denigrating, controlling, and intimidating people leads to tribalism within the team, a lack of motivation, and a systemic pattern of mediocrity. I believed that an empowered leadership at the head of Team *Merlin* would lead to an empowered crew willing to go that extra mile to win races. And as it turned out, I was right.

You can only win a sailboat race if everyone works together in harmony, like that proverbial well-oiled machine. To do that requires a collective understanding and appreciation of the mission—to win the race—and the knowledge of how to work the wind, waves, and tidal currents to best advantage to arrive at the desired outcome. Brian had never run an operation like the one we were putting together, so the experience was new to him as well. Nevertheless, I made the right choice in designating Brian as the go-to guy for everything to do with *Merlin*, including sorting through sailing résumés to find the best people for the team.

Sailboats sail fast when the bottom is perfectly smooth. Rough spots disturb the flow of water and create friction. On a cruising boat, the smoothness of the paint isn't as important, and therefore smoothness is not crucial to reach perfection. Not so with a racing yacht. We chose an expensive bottom paint that promised to deliver the top performance we were looking for, and we followed the manufacturer's advice in terms of which company would apply the paint. The recommended company was in Fort Lauderdale, so that's where the truck delivered *Merlin*.

While the yard crew worked on the paint job, Brian enlisted the North Sails team to produce a new mainsail and genoa. The mainsail on a sloop is the real driver, but the headsails up in the bow are just as important. Old sails stretch and belly. In short, they don't hold their aerodynamic shape to create the most efficient air foil. New sails simply deliver the best performance.

We'd never race without a giant spinnaker, for instance, and we wanted a genoa to extend the amount of sail area we could fly forward when sailing closer to the wind. *Merlin* spreads a lot of sail, and when the wind is up and she's sailing a close reach or close-hauled, she'll heel quite a bit. The main and jib are usually all we would need, but the "genny" was a good addition because it would allow us to extend the sail area up forward if we needed to.

When we went sailing with Bill Lee, I'd noticed that the main looked pretty beat up, almost as if it was about to fall apart. It turns out Bill didn't invest in a new main for the 2017 Transpac. The main was perhaps ten years old, in a sport where new sails are like freshly tuned engines in a Formula 1 racer. We definitely needed new sails.

The evolution of sailcloth has been incredible over the last several decades. When I started sailing as a kid, Dacron was the most common sailcloth material. It's still commonly used, but racing sails are another story. At North Sails, they use a 3Di composite material technology for racing sails that is proprietary to the company. The technical details aren't all that important here, but the core concept is that the material is ultrathin, light, and strong, and it has many of the same characteristics as a rigid aircraft wing. Less distortion of the shape translates into more speed.

North's engineers ran aerodynamic tests to determine the best shape for the sails using computer-assisted design (CAD), and the computerized system also cut *Merlin*'s new sails to the highest level of precision. I wanted to do everything possible for Team *Merlin* to win, and if that meant spending the money for state-of-the-art sails, then that was what I would do.

As is just about always the case in any sort of endeavor, problems arose as we worked hard to get the boat ready to race. We received a call from the yard manager saying that the bottom paint was peeling off because the crew had applied the paint over some older bottom paint that was still adhering to the hull. The bond wasn't holding, and they'd have to do the job over again. Of all the best-laid plans … we'd followed the paint-manufacturer's advice when selecting the company to apply the paint, and yet they'd still badly messed up the job.

When things like this happen, it's easy to lose your cool, but yelling only makes things worse. Alienating a vendor, even if the vendor was responsible for the problem (as it was in our case), will just create additional headaches when you're in the thick of a situation like we were. If you pause for a breath, count down from ten, and accept that you cannot change the past, you'll realize that you'll have time to take corrective action later. I doubt I'd rush back to this particular company for another bottom paint job. In their case, voting with my feet amounted to

> **Problems are part of life, part of business, and part of sailing. In fact, boats are constantly in need of fixing.**

the proper corrective action. Problems are part of life, part of business, and part of sailing. In fact, boats are constantly in need of fixing. It's simply the way it is. We paid the yard to take the paint off all the way down to the bare gelcoat, and to apply the new paint so it would stick. The problem was that we were quickly running out of time.

As I look back on my life before *Merlin*, everything seems to have lined up over the decades to make the present adventure with the boat possible. Obviously, choices and actions affect future outcomes. Decisions early on can have positive results, negative impacts, or very little influence on how your life goes. But choices do matter, even if they aren't going to change your life in and of themselves.

Indeed, we're not usually going to know which choices will lead to big changes, and which ones will matter little. But the choices do accumulate to make you who you are, so it's a good idea to thoughtfully consider any move before taking decisive action. Think before you act. The same is true in business and on the racecourse. Knee-jerk reactions lose races, and they cost companies lots of money in the long run when leadership fails to respond in a measured way when difficulties arise.

When I was living in Mississippi, I was keenly aware of the impacts of Hurricane Camille. The storm had hit in August 1969, a year before we arrived in Waveland, causing a twenty-four-foot storm surge along the Mississippi coast. Peak sustained winds reached 175 miles per hour. People were still rebuilding as we started our new lives there. The destruction made a deep impression on me, an impression that would indirectly chart the direction of my legal practice years later.

I think it was the empathy I felt for the good-natured and relatively poor residents of Waveland and the surrounding area that led me to ultimately choose to fight on behalf of individual policyholders in claims disputes with big insurance companies.

What I do know for sure is that I chose to specialize in a specific area of the law, and that is in helping policyholders get the payments they deserve. If a hurricane comes and the insurance company won't pay, that's when we start. Wildfires, sinkholes, tornadoes, lava flows, tsunamis, floods … you name it. If something nasty has happened to your property and you get into a dispute with the insurance company because the company won't live up to its end of the deal, that's where we step in as an advocate for the individual policyholder. On the Gulf Coast, we get a lot of hurricanes. Needless to say, I've been busy.

As I mentioned earlier, I decided to go into the law after that terrible car wreck. I began my campus life at the University of Florida with a giant white cast on my arm. I quickly joined a fraternity, and I participated in student government. Both of these pursuits helped build leadership skills, particularly my time serving as the president of my fraternity.

Animal House and other movie images aside, a fraternity house conducts itself like a small business. You have to order food, monitor inventory, do payroll, and manage events. You have to track finances, and you have to cultivate individuals to groom for leadership positions when it's time to pass the torch to the next leaders of the organization. It was a great way to learn the basics of how to efficiently manage a company as well as personnel. One of the major lessons I learned was how to effectively work with other people to achieve a common goal. You can't learn that in a classroom. You have to learn by doing.

But doing felt a long way off. A daunting seven years of school stood between me and practicing law. The prospect of so much study frankly didn't appeal to me. I wanted to move things along.

I chose to put my nose to the proverbial grindstone. I stopped sailing during the summers and took extra courses. Instead of goofing off or taking it easy, I took some good advice. I was told that winners do the hard stuff first and take it easy later. I put in the necessary effort to accelerate the launch of my legal career, graduating from college after just two and a half years. I then moved right into my studies at the Fredric G. Levin Law School at the University of Florida. Truthfully, shortening my time in school was appealing.

Most of my peers in law school were at least two years older than I was. I didn't think anything of it until I went looking for a job. When I interviewed for positions, I was aware that people thought I was too young to be a lawyer, at age twenty-three. It soon became clear that entry-level jobs at law firms meant putting a couple more years in at the law library doing research for senior attorneys.

The idea of being exiled to a musty law library for a couple more years after I'd already busted my butt to graduate early from law school didn't appeal to me. I hunted around and found a firm that was willing to take a chance on me. They promised that I'd be actively engaged in working on important cases in addition to doing research. I took the job. I'd be assisting the top attorneys in the firm in their work representing big insurance companies.

The work was hard. I put in long hours finding ways for insurance companies to win disputes against their own customers. I learned a lot, but I wasn't happy about my job. I didn't go home with a smile on my face after winning a case, because I knew it usually meant that someone just got shafted. And I'd helped do it.

I learned almost immediately that insurance companies always know their rights. Policyholders often don't. If you or your attorney don't know your rights, mistakes will happen. Judgments may be unjust or totally unwarranted. Claims can go unpaid when they should be paid in full.

Time passed. I grew increasingly discontented, not only with the work but with the low level of compensation the insurance companies were willing to pay attorneys. One day, I stopped at a car-repair shop and saw a sign saying that the mechanics were all paid in excess of fifty bucks an hour. The company was trying to make the point that its employees were well paid, and that fair compensation would translate into superior service. There's a lot of validity to that. At any rate, one of our insurance clients wanted to pay forty-five dollars per hour to handle cases.

I thought, *Why would anybody go to law school if you can get a job that pays better fresh out of high school?*

It dawned on me that I was representing the wrong side. The policyholders had no one to advocate for them. At the time when I started Merlin Law Group in 1985, no attorneys (to my knowledge) were specializing in representing policyholders in property-claim disputes with insurance companies. It was such a highly specialized part of the law that it had been overlooked, at least in the state of Florida. The insurance companies had top-flight talent. I thought policyholders should as well.

Insurance is one of the only products that we're forced to buy. If you have a mortgage, you'll have to buy homeowner's insurance. If you own a car, you can't legally roll down the road without car insurance. The problem is that most people don't know what they're paying for when they buy insurance because they don't read and understand the policy. Heck, sometimes I don't even read some of my policies. As a consequence, customers don't know their rights and the insurance company can often find ways to get out of paying claims. Most attorneys don't even know how to interpret the complicated and convoluted language used in insurance policies. Sometimes I think the language is written that way on purpose.

As these ideas were churning in my head, opportunity came calling. A client, Gale Porter, was fighting the local telephone company over a rate dispute. The case involved the client's acquisition of special time/weather telephone lines from the telephone company as part of the overall breakup of the large monopoly. My client's customers could call a number to get the time or the local weather, and an ad would come up as well. The advertising dollars were supposed to generate sufficient profit to make the purchase of the lines worthwhile. After the purchase, however, the telephone company turned around and charged three times the previous rate for the lines.

Porter sued, saying that the rate increase was unfair, that it was almost retaliatory, in that the telephone company seemed to be getting back at the client for being part of the breakup. If a rate adjustment couldn't be arranged, the client would lose the investment and go out of business. I spent hundreds of hours on the case.

We won.

And this time I really did go home with a big smile on my face. I knew I'd made a positive difference in the world. One that I was proud about. That drove home the point that I wasn't happy working for the insurance companies. I had to get out of there. I just wasn't sure how.

Not long afterward, that client, Gale Porter, called me to say he had set aside some office space for me in his building. He'd known I was interested in starting my own law practice, and that I wanted to represent policyholders. I hurried over to see what the client had in mind. The windowless office was tiny, but it could be mine at an affordable rent. If I lived with friends to save money, ate nothing but ramen noodles and cheap hot dogs, and drove an old beater, I figured I could make a go of this crazy venture.

It was sobering to be told I would probably fail, and that I should stay safe and stick with the big firm and follow a traditional career path.

When I told some people about my plans, they said at twenty-six I was too young to open my own practice. I weighed their advice carefully. It was sobering to be told I would probably fail, and that I should stay safe and stick with the big firm and follow a traditional career path. In the end, I decided to take the risk of starting my own law firm. I intuitively knew that if I didn't, I would probably regret it for the rest of my life. At the very least, I would have been left wondering what would've or could've been; not a comforting place to be on an emotional and psychological level.

If you're not passionate about what you do, what's the point of doing it? I understand that many of us feel we don't have choices in what we do, but I've never believed that. Some studies say that 71 percent of us hate our jobs. To me, that's sad. We spend the majority of our time at work. We might as well do something we love. Otherwise, we're wasting our lives, and we're not realizing our true potential if we don't even try to get there.

I recall conversations with my dad about why it's so important to follow your passion, to make the choice to move forward with a dream instead of ignoring it or making excuses as to why you can't make that dream a reality. My dad used a hypothetical example of a bridge tender to make his point. If all you want to do is open and close a bridge when a boat comes along, watch the seagulls, and enjoy the natural setting, then choosing a career as a bridge tender makes sense. You know you will never earn piles of cash, and you don't care. You're happy doing what you love.

When I hire people to join the Merlin legal team, I want to know what they're passionate about. I ask them what their dream is, and I tell them I want to work with them to make their dream come true. It might sound a little corny, but I want the team member to feel invested in the firm, appreciated for his or her unique talents, and sustained in a supportive culture that encourages personal and professional advancement on a continual basis.

When I asked one attorney what her dream was, she said she wanted to be a judge. We tailored her workload to put her on the right committees to get on a trajectory for a judgeship. Another attorney said he wanted to be the governor of Florida. We set up his job to give him exposure in political circles. He eventually was nominated as the Democratic candidate for Florida attorney general. He lost that race, but he got to pursue his dream. That's all that really matters, isn't it?

I credit my dad for instilling in me a solid grasp of what's needed to be an effective leader. We'd talk about what makes a good skipper, and sometimes he'd take me with him on a short cruise in the Gulf aboard a coast guard ship. I saw how the crew respected him, how he made sure to cultivate leaders in the various departments, and how he gave junior officers opportunities to learn new skills that would enable them to advance to positions of higher rank. He led by example, always calmly communicating what he wanted done without being a Captain Bligh.

As the law firm grew and I hired more and more people, I tried to lead like my dad. I wasn't always successful. In the early days, my management style was sometimes not the best. I'd be too demanding, and I'd get frustrated with employees when things went wrong or weren't accomplished fast enough. Lawyers are typically some of the worst leaders, in part because we tend to think we know it all, and in part because leadership is not taught in law school.

If you google "leadership styles," you'll find tons of stuff on the various types of leaders. Autocratic, charismatic, transactional, trans-formational, servant, democratic, inspirational, and laissez-faire leadership styles are all discussed at length. My position is that effective leaders fall into any number of styles.

> **Good leaders build people up, and bad leaders tear them down.**

In my opinion, leadership is about what you *do*, not your leadership style. Good leaders build people up, and bad leaders tear them down. Good leaders have a vision for the company's growth. Bad leaders stumble along, always putting out fires, many of their own making. Good leaders stand above the fray of the day-to-day, in favor of guiding the ship into the future with a steady hand and a solid understanding of how to get to the desired destination. Good leaders communicate clearly, and bad leaders don't.

I learned after failures to say, "You might consider doing it this way." I now never say it's my way or the highway, except with issues of ethics, but I had to learn that strategy. It didn't come naturally. I doubt there is such a thing as a born leader, but maybe there is. If so, they're as rare as hen's teeth.

That first year in private law practice was tough. As the proverbial chief cook and bottle washer, I had to do absolutely everything. Within two weeks or so of hanging up my shingle, I got two referrals that led to positive cash flow. I wasn't as busy as I wanted to be, but I was confident that the work would pick up if I just kept at it. More important … I was happy.

Being on my own in the big bad world of the law was exhilarating. I was smart enough to know I had my limits in terms of experience, and I also knew that I'd become a better lawyer with experience. I believed if I worked hard and won, more cases would come, which is exactly what happened. I also knew that specialization was critical, and that specialization in an aspect of the law few did would position me for probable success.

Early successes led to more referrals, and I was definitely on my way. Best of all, I was doing something I felt passionate about. I wanted to help people win cases against big insurance companies that didn't want to hold up their end of the bargain. I proceeded knowing deep in my heart that I'd done the right thing in quitting that first job. I'll always be grateful to the leadership at the firm for giving me a chance. I've paid the favor forward hundreds of times since then when I've given others a chance to succeed and lead happy and rewarding lives.

Giving back is simply the right thing to do, both on a personal and business level. Being a good corporate citizen is as important as being a good private citizen. Like it or not, we're all in the same boat, so we might as well all pitch in to make the world better for everybody instead of just looking out for our own best interests.

Getting back to *Merlin*, I chose Brian Malone as the team leader for many reasons. One of them was his clear passion for sailing. It's in his blood. He can't get enough of it. He earns his living as a sailmaker. He's around sailing all day long, and that's just fine with him. Passionate people tend to win at what they love doing best. I was looking for a winner, and I found one in Brian.

More time passed. It was now mid-February, and the paint job still wasn't done. I was beginning to wonder if we would actually get to do the Cuba race. I tried not to think about it as I went about my work at the law firm. You can control many things, but you can't control how another company does business. You can only choose never to deal with the company again if a problem isn't properly addressed and resolved.

Finally, just about a week before the race, the paint job was done. The delivery crew sailed *Merlin* from Fort Lauderdale, around the Florida Keys, and on up to St. Pete. The rush was on to get in at least some practice racing before we shoved off for Cuba to do the real thing … my first important ocean race with *Merlin*.

5

VICTORY

I LEANED BACK in the cockpit, glanced around at the sailboats in the slips beside us in the marina, and surveyed the crew gathered together for our first practice session aboard *Merlin*. Everyone looked serious, intent, and excited to be part of the Merlin Yacht Racing team for the St. Petersburg–Habana race. I was glad to have them in my corner.

Among the more experienced crew members was James Clappier, a seasoned ocean racer from Richmond, California, who would serve as the bowman. Chris Watts, of Santa Cruz, would stand as the mainsail trimmer. Chris had sailed *Merlin* with Bill Lee. He knew the boat better than anyone else in the crew. For that matter, most of us didn't know much about the boat except Chris, and except for those members of the crew who had just sailed her from the boatyard in Fort Lauderdale to St. Pete.

The situation was far from ideal. The boat had only just arrived from Fort Lauderdale, and the race was two days away. Team members barely knew each other well, and we'd had no time to practice and hone our racing chops. We had a fantastic boat. Indeed, we were the fastest-rated vessel, and yet we were starting out at a distinct disadvantage.

You can have the best boat in the world, but if you don't have the right team to sail her, you're not likely to win. I knew deep down from my one-design skippering days that the quality and training of the crew matter. A lot. So does the team you work with in the boardroom or on the shop floor. Training and practicing are vital to success.

> You can have the best boat in the world, but if you don't have the right team to sail her, you're not likely to win.

I could have come aboard on this first practice day laden with negativity. I could have still been steaming over the botched paint job that had caused such lengthy delays, delays that were now affecting my ability to win the Cuba race because the team had so little time to learn how to work together to make the boat go as fast as possible. I could have told myself that the lack of practice time meant we would likely lose the race, but I didn't do that.

Negative self-talk just brings you down. People can sense it if you feel negative, so that kind of negative self-talk can bring your entire team down with you if you walk around oozing negativity all day long. No, I learned long ago that positive self-talk has the opposite effect of negative self-talk. A positive, can-do outlook brings your own personal attitude up instead of down. It has the same effect on the team.

I aimed for a positive, buoyant, and upbeat attitude as Brian and I worked through the hassles with the boatyard, and as we sorted through all the other things that needed sorting through to get us where we were at this point. One of the keys to succeeding is keeping a clear vision of what you want to achieve. If you can see the victory in your mind's eye, as opposed to merely hoping you'll succeed, you are more likely to actually win at whatever you're trying to do.

For me, the Cuba race was the first of five planned for 2018, and I wanted to win every regatta. Nobody races to lose. When I pictured myself standing at the awards ceremony at the Hemingway International Marina to accept the trophy for first-to-finish and line honors, accomplishing the objective seemed somehow more real, more achievable. One of our biggest goals was to set a course record, which was quite possible with a speedster like *Merlin*.

Challenges are part of life in general, and they're also part of winning a yacht race. Expect to face challenges in any worthwhile effort, and expect to face setbacks as well. We'd overcome the obstacles with teamwork, patience (as much as I could muster), and a positive attitude. We'd committed to the race, and we all were in it to place in the money. It's that kind of determination—the will to take active, purposeful steps to achieve the goal—that sets winners apart from losers. Losers make excuses for not acting on their dreams. They are typically adrift in their personal lives and in business, and they are usually unhappy and reek of infectious negativity.

Brian stood near the wheel at the aft end of the long slender cockpit, one hand resting on the backstay. "This is a powerful boat," he said, "and she deserves the utmost respect. Everything about her is big. I know most of you have never sailed a boat as big as she is before, so I want to tell you what to expect."

Brian explained that the forces on the sails and rig would be exponentially more powerful than anything we had ever experienced before. James Clappier held up his hand, showing us the stub of one of his fingers. "Lost it to a winch," he said as casually as if he'd just ordered a sandwich.

I noticed some of the crew looked a bit pale under their tans. This speech and demonstration caught my attention as well.

"Count on one thing," Brian continued. "Everything is going to be faster than you're used to. The boat is lively and wet, and she can be tough to handle. If you don't know how something works, or if you have any questions, we want you to ask instead of making a bad mistake that could end up getting you hurt. There are no stupid questions on boats. As the saying goes, 'There are bold sailors, but there are no *old* bold sailors.'"

As Brian and Chris showed us how everything worked, Brian's cautionary words drove home to me just how serious the ocean racing business can be. If you screw up in my niche area of the law, people can get hurt financially. But nobody dies or is maimed for life. If you make the wrong decision on an ocean racing sailboat, the entire crew can be lost, and sometimes never be heard from again.

As we cast off the lines and motored out of the marina, waves of anticipation washed over me. *We are actually doing this,* I thought. *Amazing!*

Once we were out in Tampa Bay, we fumbled through setting the main and the jib in the light southwesterly breeze of eight to ten knots. I kept the bow into the wind long enough for Chris to finish raising the huge black mainsail. It thundered as it luffed. I eased the bow slightly off the wind and the sail filled. Brian killed the engine, and all went blissfully silent.

The enormity of what we were about to do really hit home. I silently wondered if I'd made the right decision in buying the boat. Had I bitten off more than I could chew?

Self-doubt is natural. We all have second thoughts. The trick is to banish the doubts and proceed according to plan, as long as you are sure you thought the plan out to the best of your ability before you got started. We'd done our homework with *Merlin*. It was just that we lacked the time to do what I knew we needed to do in terms of crew practice.

I headed slightly up into the wind, luffing the main, as the crew raised the giant jib. Both sails, all nearly two thousand square feet of them, flogged and flapped, making a sound like gunfire. I gently eased her off to get on a faster point of sail, and the boat took off in her usual rocket-like style. All things considered, the set went well enough, though we certainly weren't all functioning like a well-oiled machine.

As a crew, we had to stop, think things through, and then address each task one by one. The best crews who have sailed together for many years almost act like a single organism, working together without having to communicate much. Everyone knows his or her job, and the team handles challenges without having to reinvent the wheel each time. Successful leaders in all endeavors cultivate teams that do the same thing.

Time was so limited that we only had a couple of hours to practice, which gave us just enough time to figure out the basics of how everything worked. We returned to the dock pleased with how well the boat sailed, and sobered by her immense power. This was a boat we'd have to learn by sailing. We had a few more hours of practice, and the next day we set sail for Havana.

The waterfront was alive with spectators clustered on and near the St. Petersburg Municipal Pier. Small craft of every type maneuvered around the fleet as I steered *Merlin* toward the starting line, moving at five or six knots in the light southerly wind with the main and jib set and drawing fair. The mood aboard was festive. We were in the race to win, of course, but we also were out there to have some serious fun.

I glanced to port as I eased *Merlin* off to pass a spectator boat, and there was *Chips Ahoy!* … my fifty-two-foot motor yacht. She was pacing us, her gray hull and modernistic lines cutting a fine form as she held steady abeam. Her decks were crowded with all my good friends, each one wearing a pointy wizard hat that Donice had found. We felt it only fitting to carry on the Bill Lee wizard tradition.

"They look like they're having a blast," I said to no one in particular. "Here, Brian, take the helm for a minute."

I hurried below and grabbed my own wizard hat, put it on, and went back up on deck. Everyone was laughing and waving while trying to pay attention to the start. Time was ticking by fast, and the start was about to happen. The mood aboard *Merlin* changed. We were all business now. Brian, who agreed to serve as tactician, held a stopwatch in one hand as he counted down the seconds to the start.

"One minute, fifty-two seconds," Brian said.

"Ready about?" I said, issuing the customary pretack warning to the crew in the cockpit.

"Ready about!" the trimmers on the jib and main replied.

"Helm's alee!" I said, and I gently brought the bow through the eye of the wind as the jib trimmer to leeward let go the sheet. The trimmer on the new leeward side brought the sheet home, trimming the sail to draw fair as I came around to the new heading. The big main swung over on its own. Chris tweaked the trim.

The racecourse was crowded, and we had to keep our wits about us to avoid running down a spectator boat while we tried to time the start so we'd cross the line right at the gun. Sadly, in part due to wind shifts and in part due to utter inexperience with the boat, we tacked back to cross the line late by about fifteen seconds.

Hiding my disappointment from the team, I continued to steer through the fleet. The boat was moving well, despite the light air, and we could all see that we were pulling ahead. One by one we began passing boats, large and small. The Sunshine Skyway Bridge drew closer. The fleet fell farther and farther behind.

"You know how they say something like bringing a knife to a gunfight?" Chris asked. He laughed, shook his head. "Well, you just brought a bazooka to a knife fight! You better take a good look at the fleet now because you won't be seeing it again until we get to Havana."

We had the water to ourselves as we sailed under the bridge and followed the channel into the Gulf of Mexico. Forecasters had called for light winds. I prayed to the wind gods that we wouldn't be becalmed. We weren't taking *Merlin* on a Loop Current hunt like we did with Dave's boat. We planned to head nearly due south straight for Havana, keeping fairly close to the west coast of Florida in the hope of picking up a stronger shore breeze as the day went on. At dusk, we intended to head farther offshore to catch whatever sea breeze we could.

The wind wheezed, puffed, stopped, started, wheezed again, and, quite frankly, started to drive me crazy. The boat moved steadily onward when there was wind, and she stopped when the wind died, which it did with frustrating regularity.

At times, there are things you just can't control, whether it's in life, business, or sailboat racing. This was one of those times, and I had to tamp down my irritation about something I could do nothing about. It does no good to scream at Mother Nature. She's not going to listen.

As the sun went down, the humidity went up. Dew covered everything above decks. It dripped off the rigging, off the boom, off the sails. Every time we tacked, buckets of water splashed off the sails, soaking us as if we were in a mini rain squall. Disgusted, I went below to get some shut-eye. It was hot in the cabin, making it difficult to sleep. An hour later, I came back on deck and asked Brian where we were.

"Oh, we're about in the same place we were an hour ago," he said, sighing. "Pretty frustrating."

"Tell me about it."

"Hey, at least we're still way ahead of the fleet," Brian said. "They're stuck just like we are."

Cold comfort. We'd barely moved a quarter mile in an hour. This was like a repeat of the previous Cuba race, and I was not happy about it, at least as far as wind conditions were concerned. I also knew darn well that there would be no bongo drums, Led Zeppelin, or ice-cold champagne aboard this time. We were out to win, not to party.

Later, people watching our position on the race-tracking app told me they thought we'd run aground, which would have been a possibility, since *Merlin* draws eleven feet and there are some shoals off the Keys that she could easily have hit if the navigator wasn't paying enough attention to our position relative to the shoals. We just weren't moving much, and so the silhouette of the boat that showed up on the computer screen looked like it was stationary. I kissed any hope of setting a course record goodbye.

We didn't throw up our hands and quit because things weren't going right. We kept trying to squeeze out every bit of speed the boat could give us. The on-watch crew perched their bottoms on the windward rail, legs hanging down on the outside of the hull, "hiking" the boat flatter. The added weight of human ballast helped keep the boat sailing as flat as possible. When a boat heels, or tilts over, more of the hull is in the water, which adds wetted surface that then increases friction. Friction makes boats go slower. Less friction makes them go faster. While hiking out wasn't really necessary in the current conditions, the crew did it anyway.

We also made sure the bilge was bone dry. Every gallon of water weighs eight pounds. That adds up to a lot of extra weight if you've got even a small amount of water in the bilge of a boat as big as *Merlin*.

Time passed. We inched our way closer to Cuba. The crew dived into the watch schedule, and I realized that the routine of standing watch for four hours before having a break of four hours added a sense of predictability to an unpredictable environment. Stability is necessary in life. We are creatures of habit, and when our routines are disturbed, the world doesn't feel quite right. Too much change can feel chaotic. That's one reason why some people avoid change at all costs. They've got their routines, and they're stickin' to 'em. Yet too much stability can cause you to stagnate. Challenges, on the other hand, force you to act. Challenges keep you on your toes. Too much stability can lull you into complacency and inertia. It's all about finding the right balance, as it is with everything in life.

The night watches were some of my favorite, both aboard *Patience* and aboard *Merlin* in this latest race. The natural splendor of the sea beneath a sky spangled with stars, a crescent moon shining dull white, a swath of clouds to windward that blots out the heavens—it all captivated me. It still does even now, after putting thousands of miles under the keel since that time. I recall sitting in the cockpit and just admiring the beauty around me as we loped along toward Havana, and I felt small in the presence of such magnificence.

As I listened to the sound of the waves gently swishing and heaving, with the dim red light of the navigation station below visible through the open companionway, I thought back to how far I'd come since I'd first opened Merlin Law Group in 1985.

We started out as a one-man operation, and now the firm employs about 175 people, sixty-three of whom are top-flight attorneys all specializing in advocating for individuals and businesses in claims disputes with their insurance companies. We now have offices all over the country, but we didn't get there overnight. Looking back on it, I'd have to say it was the case of the missing cows that really put us on the map in the mid-1990s.

On August 24, 1992, Hurricane Andrew came ashore in present-day Miami-Dade County, Florida, as a cat 5 monster with wind gusts of more than 165 miles per hour. By the time the dust had settled, the storm had killed sixty-five people in the Bahamas, South Florida, and Louisiana, and it had caused $27.3 billion in property damage. More than 65,000 homes were totally destroyed, and 124,000 others were damaged. No other hurricane would come close to Andrew's death and destruction until Hurricane Katrina hit the Gulf Coast in August 2005.

South Florida was particularly hard hit. The devastation was widespread, and the insurance industry was paying out huge sums in property-damage claims. One such claimant was Miami-based Farm Stores. The company began in 1935 as the Land O' Sun Dairies, selling milk, ice cream, and butter in the South Florida market. Over time, the operation expanded, and in 1957 the owners followed the burgeoning drive-through trend, spurred in part by the explosive growth of McDonald's, which had opened two years earlier in San Bernardino, California.

Think of Farm Stores as a drive-through supermarket, where you could pull up to a window and buy fresh dairy and produce. It really was just like you'd order a Big Mac. These stores sprouted up virtually everywhere in South Florida, and Hurricane Andrew took many of them out.

The Farm Stores logo was, appropriately enough, a white cow with black splotches on its back. I believe it was of the Holstein breed, the most common type found on dairy farms. The Holstein dominated the signage advertising the stores, and people loved it, calling it *la pequeña vaca*, or the little cow. As you drove down the highway, you'd see a tall brown pole with an arrow pointing toward the store. Atop the Farm Stores sign stood the black-and-white cow, its muzzle facing the road. You really couldn't miss it. That cow was more noticeable than Mickey D's Golden Arches. No matter how well you build a cow sign, it's not going to stand up to the likes of a Hurricane Andrew. There were cows down all over South Florida.

A group of investors acquired the chain that same year. It was an unlucky time to have bought Farm Stores, but just like everyone else in the path of the storm who suffered damage, they filed a claim with their insurance company. The company paid the minimum on the policy. Not finding the settlement offer fair, Farm Stores got me involved in 1994.

Very few firms were specializing in my niche area of the law in the mid-1990s. In the wake of Hurricane Andrew, I added more attorneys, and I put a couple of my best people on the Farm Stores case. It was a big case for me and the firm, and I knew it.

While the case with the insurance company was in dispute, efforts to reopen the damaged Farm Stores continued. By the time I got involved, most of the stores were up and running. Yet sales after the storm were down significantly, despite the fact that the stores had been rebuilt and were currently serving customers. No one knew why, but it seemed pretty obvious that the decline in business had something to do with Hurricane Andrew.

Often, success in life and business comes about through serendipity, and that's what occurred with the Farm Stores case. It just so happened that my ex-wife, Kim, was an expert litigator in cases involving eminent domain, where a state or local government can take property for the greater good of the public. One of the big areas of dispute in many of her cases involved how the loss of signage in businesses embroiled in these sorts of clashes caused financial damage. It occurred to me that the decline in Farm Stores revenue subsequent to the storm might just have something to do with the signs. Not all the stores had replaced their cow signs yet, because the sign companies were still overwhelmed with orders even two years after the storm.

My position was that a store could be rebuilt and serving customers, but if the road sign was missing, the store had not returned to normal operations. Therefore, the business was still interrupted as a result of the storm, despite the fact that the stores themselves were operational. I admit that it was a novel approach. The insurance company claimed that the signs didn't figure into settling a business-interruption claim. The stores had been rebuilt, and that was that.

I recalled that Kim had obtained the services of a professor at the University of South Florida who specialized in the economic and microeconomic impact that road signage and marketing have on business profitability. I called him and asked if he would study the Farm Stores case. He agreed. It turned out that the stores with signs up were doing between 25 to 30 percent more business than the stores that did not have their signs up. I argued that the stores without the signs had not been truly rebuilt, and that the business continued to be interrupted.

Naturally, the insurance company disagreed. Finally, in 1996, the insurance company settled. The settlement amount was confidential, and the case did not get any press. It did get a lot of attention in legal circles, however, because my clients asked me to contribute $25,000 of my fee to the University of Miami engineering and law schools, which I did. Some of my peers thought this was pretty funny because I'm a University of Florida guy all the way. At any rate, referrals came in even faster after that.

It's intriguing how serendipitous life can be. I never would have thought of the possibility that the missing signs could have played a role in the decline in Farm Stores business after

> Sometimes things just come together, but you've got to be alert and observant to encourage positive outcomes even in difficult situations.

Hurricane Andrew if it hadn't been for my listening to Kim talk about how companies were losing their signs to eminent domain, and that those lost signs were costing businesses a lot of money. Further, I never would have known about the economist from the University of South Florida. Sometimes things just come together, but you've got to be alert and observant to encourage positive outcomes even in difficult situations.

Serendipity played a big part in my buying *Merlin*. If I hadn't been looking for a boat to sail with my dad on the Newport-Bermuda race, and if I hadn't been on my iPad looking almost the same day Bill Lee put *Merlin* up for sale, I probably wouldn't have been in a position to buy her. And the boat wouldn't have been up for sale if Bill hadn't reacquired her in 2016 to run the 2017 Transpac with plans to sell her after the race. Luck plays a role in all our lives in one way or another. So does serendipity.

The wind piped up a bit as we passed the Dry Tortugas, and it increased as we approached the Gulf Stream. Finally, *Merlin* was sailing fast enough to keep me happy. I grinned as I checked the tracking app and saw how far out in front of the fleet we were, and the lead was getting more pronounced as the boat sped up. As we sailed into the confused seas that are almost always present in the Gulf Stream, I turned to Dave Kilcoyne and asked, "Remember the return trip last year?"

Dave laughed and said, "How could I forget that? That was an awesome ride. Scary too!"

And it had been both. After a slow 2017 Cuba race, a frontal system swept in with strong easterly winds for the fleet's return north. An east wind against the east-setting Gulf Stream meant the wind opposed the current. When the wind opposes the current, the battle between the two kicks up tall, steep breaking waves that can be deadly. Many skippers postponed leaving and flew home, figuring that they'd come back to get their boats later. Others left and reported heavy seas. We delayed our departure for a day, hoping the weather would improve. It would be just five of us on the boat on the way back because Brian, our only experienced offshore sailor, had to fly home early.

At dinner that night, we discussed whether we should stay or go. The winds seemed to be easing, and that was good news. But the conditions were still rough. Ultimately, we all decided to see how things stood in the morning. We awoke bright and early, and checked the weather report. Conditions had indeed eased … a little. We decided to go.

The coast of Cuba near Havana tends to shelter you from the full effects of a strong easterly wind. For one thing, you're in the lee on the west side of the island in a wind shadow of sorts. Looking out at the water beyond the reef, the waves appeared to be no more than a few feet tall. *Patience* could handle that, we thought.

About five miles out, we emerged from the lee. The wind increased and seas began to build. I was getting nervous, and I could tell the rest of the crew was too. As the skipper, I had to put a brave face on the situation, exuding confidence when I knew I was totally out of my league in those conditions. The wind reached twenty to twenty-five knots sustained, with higher gusts. On the Beaufort wind scale, which is something like the Saffir–Simpson hurricane wind scale, we were in a near gale. In a near gale, you'll encounter winds between twenty-eight and thirty-three knots, with thirteen- to fourteen-foot seas. That's nothing to sneeze at, even on a stable boat like Dave's.

When we entered the Gulf Stream, with the easterly wind blowing westward against the current, the waves built to twenty feet and began to break with vicious-looking white crests that roared over the bow as the boat surged through the boiling cauldron of the stream under a roller-reefed main and jib. Two of the crew were incapacitated with seasickness, lying curled up in the fetal position on their bunks below decks, leaving only three of us to sail the boat.

"You've been out in waves like this before, right?" asked Dave's wife, Karena.

A particularly large comber swept in, giving us a salty bath. Spray flew halfway up to the spreaders as *Patience* plunged on.

"Oh, yeah!" I said. "I've been out in this before. No problem. We'll get across okay."

I didn't bother to tell her that the only other time I'd ever been in sea conditions like those was when I was a kid and my dad took me on a short cruise on a two-hundred-foot coast guard vessel. That had been a long time ago.

Just then, we started hearing Mayday calls from another yacht fighting it out with the stream like we were. Earlier, we'd seen a Farr 395 away off to starboard. A fine racing boat, and certainly much lighter than *Patience,* the sleek sloop would drop down in the trough of a wave, and we'd lose sight of the hull. On the crests, we watched the crew all hiked out on the windward side. It occurred to me that they must have felt more like they were in a submarine than a yacht. The waves frequently washed over them.

As the drama with the boat in trouble played out on the VHF radio, I babied *Patience*, not wanting to press her too hard in case I broke something important, like the mast. If something popped in those conditions, we'd be in a bad position, given that we were both short-handed and inexperienced. While I was pretending to know what I was doing at the helm in those atrocious seas, I heard the panic in the voice of the distressed boat's skipper as he relayed what was happening over the VHF radio. Although the skipper tried to keep his cool, it was a sobering moment. I could tell he was really scared, and I felt great compassion and concern for him and his crew.

So, now we were in the Gulf Stream again, heading to Cuba just a year or so after that harrowing return trip. The rest of the second day and evening passed uneventfully. As we approached Havana at dawn the next morning, the sun peeked over the horizon, revealing the beautiful tropical island, lush with green heights. The Gulf Stream had set us to the east, and we had to sail close to the wind to make our westing to the harbor entrance. The closer we got, the higher we had to point.

"Try pointing her a little higher," Chris said. "I don't think she'll lose that much speed, and we'll be heading more toward Havana."

We were flying the big genny Brian had made for the race. The huge sail was a wonder. Even with the light wind of about six knots, *Merlin* was doing nine knots, and we were sailing about as close to the wind as we could get without stalling the boat. At this point, we were about ninety miles ahead of the nearest boat in the fleet, which was all jammed up around the Dry Tortugas. Chris noticed that the crew had begun to get a bit complacent, as if they didn't have to work so hard because we had such a sizable lead.

"Gentlemen," Chris said, "are we racing or are we riding?"

He meant that we had to keep on pushing right to the end. As the highest-rated boat in the fleet, *Merlin* had quite a time handicap. That meant we had to sail as fast as we could, or a smaller boat could still beat us on corrected time. One boat from New Orleans was just minutes behind us on corrected time. We could still lose corrected time honors in our class if we didn't keep hustling.

As the sun rose higher, we streaked into the channel leading to Hemingway International Marina. It was a beautiful morning I'll never forget. We finished the race on February 28, 2018, with an elapsed time of one day, nineteen hours, thirty-one minutes, and fifty seconds. We were an astonishing twelve hours ahead of a catamaran. It's a given that multihulls sail much faster than monohulls, in part because a big cat has a lot less wetted surface than a monohull of similar size. That's why the cats, or "gunboats" as they are sometimes called, get put in their own classes. Still, despite the vast differences between the two types of sailboats, skippers of monohulls get quite a kick out of besting their multihulled brethren. I certainly did.

The fleet started to straggle in while we were celebrating over dinner that night, drinking rum and having the time of our lives. It was touch and go with that boat from New Orleans, but we did win line honors by a couple of minutes. Our corrected time for the race was two days, three hours, ten minutes, and thirty-two seconds. Obviously, we won first-to-finish honors as well.

As we savored our victory, I lifted my glass and said, "Here's to *Merlin*!"

"Cheers!" everyone said.

We all clinked glasses. We toasted Bill Lee too. Fast really *is* fun!

6

NEWPORT

THE SMOOTH WATERS off Newport's Castle Hill teemed with boats gathered at the start of the fifty-first running of the 635-mile biennial Newport-Bermuda race. The colorful sails of the competitors and spectator boats contrasted against the cliffs on the west side of Aquidneck Island. The island is home to Newport Harbor, which became a vital trading and fishing port in Rhode Island's Narragansett Bay not long after the village was founded in 1639.

Now the city of Newport is known for its vibrant sailing community. In fact, Newport bills itself as the "sailing capital of the world." Other yachting meccas might dispute that claim, but the venue did serve as the staging ground for the America's Cup races for more than fifty years. That has to count for something.

As I steered *Merlin* through the chaos near the starting line, I noted that the tops of the hills to the east were adorned with lush green manicured lawns, palatial estates, and stands of stately deciduous trees that had probably been there since the Gilded Age, when Newport reigned as the supreme summer retreat for the American aristocracy.

I'd sampled a taste of the high society of the city during my visit to the New York Yacht Club's Newport clubhouse, and at the prerace parties we attended.

We had a total of fourteen sailors aboard *Merlin*, some of whom had raced with the team to Cuba and Isla Mujeres in Mexico earlier in the 2018 racing season. Among them were Brian Malone and Chris Watts. Those guys might not make their living as full-time professional sailors (few people can—like the incredible James Clappier, whom I'd also like to recognize), but they brought a wealth of ocean racing experience to the party.

As always, I was happy to have people around me who knew what they were doing. The Newport-Bermuda race can be challenging. You have to have a good boat and crew to do it with any degree of safety. If you get into trouble out there, you're pretty much on your own because you're out of range of the coast guard rescue choppers, either from the United States or from Bermuda. Strict safety rules apply in this race.

Bill, my eighty-three-year-old dad, was on board for the race. Indeed, taking him on this race was the main reason why I'd bought the boat. A former admiral in the United States Coast Guard, Dad had sailed to Bermuda as a cadet aboard USS *Eagle* in 1950. The romance of sailing a tall ship to beautiful Bermuda made a big impression on him, and when he had the chance to sail in the Newport-Bermuda race in 1954 as a cadet and in 1956 as a graduate, he went for it without hesitation.

I recalled many conversations with my dad about those races. His excitement was as palpable as his wistfulness when he talked about them. Sailing had been new to him in the coast guard, but he took to it immediately.

He loved the teamwork and camaraderie of racing one-designs with his classmates, and he remains an avid sailor to this day. The current race was special for both of us. For him, it was a real bucket list item to settle, and for me it was a chance to give my dad a pinnacle adventure in a long life lived with honor, humor, humility, compassion, courage, respect, and, most of all, love. I hadn't raced with Dad since I was nineteen, so it was pretty special to look over and see keen attention lighting his face.

Merlin jockeyed back and forth away from the starting line as we waited for our divisional start. The start of the race was staggered. It would almost have to be, what with 169 boats in the racing fleet. The slowest-rated boats started first, heading out in waves, almost like an assault force on an amphibious beach landing.

We were in the next-to-last group to go. Given that the race-spectator party had begun before the first start about two hours earlier, the celebrating had been well underway by the time we showed up at the line. As I stood at the helm, I heard the music at a rollicking pool party on the grounds of the Newport Yacht Club. Announcers emceed from atop Castle Hill, reporting on each boat as it passed for the thousands of merry spectators. Soon, it was our turn to go.

"And here comes *Merlin*!" the announcer ashore told the crowd.

We were a bit busy at the time, but we later heard that the announcer gave the spectators a short history lesson about *Merlin*. It makes me feel proud to know that the boat is so well known and so well regarded. Indeed, after we'd finished the Mexico race earlier in the 2018 racing season, a local kid about ten years old had come down to the dock to admire the boat. He knew all about her. We invited him aboard. His eyes widened by the second as he looked at the giant winches, the wheel that was taller than he was, and the towering mast that seemed to scrape the sky.

The start of a sailboat race is tense. You try to cross the starting line just as the starting gun is fired, or just after it. If you cross before the gun, you've got to go back and restart, losing precious time that can make or break a race. Ideally, the crew works as one, each knowing his or her job. There isn't (or shouldn't be) shouting and confusion. Of course, there usually is some of that. Things happen really fast as you ease sheets to fall off the wind, or you trim up tight to sail close-hauled, and then tack to spin around and line up for the gun. I gripped the wheel as we headed to the starting line. As the seconds ticked on, I knew we weren't going to make it on time.

Boom! The loud report of the starting cannon echoed off the cliffs.

Crap, I thought. *Missed it by seconds!*

We were late on the start, and worse, we'd gotten boxed in behind the other boats in our division just off the line. The boats were all vying for clear wind, and we were getting pinched. When a boat gets upwind of you, her sails can blanket yours if she comes close to your wind. One of my competitors tried to do just that. The last thing I wanted was to lose my wind. Even a temporary blanketing means slow. Slow is not fun.

I didn't buy *Merlin* to go slow. I bought her to do this race in particular with my dad, and I bought her to win every race she ran, no matter what. You can't always win, but you can always try to win. It's the trying hard, *really* hard, that matters most. With that in mind, I shrugged off the bad start and focused on the task at hand.

> You can't always win, but you can always try to win. It's the trying hard, *really* hard, that matters most.

Seeing an opening to port, we came around onto that tack, picking up speed as we sailed fast close-hauled into Rhode Island Sound. The crew, all dressed in foul-weather gear, hustled to the windward rail after we settled onto the tack. They hiked out, projecting their body weight as far from the center of the boat to windward as possible to improve the boat's trim and speed.

Merlin displaces only 24,000 pounds. Say each crew member weighs 150 pounds. If you put ten members on the rail, that's 1,500 pounds of live ballast that can be moved around to change the trim of the boat. Relative to the overall displacement, the crew placement really does make a difference in a boat like *Merlin*. I can tell you from experience that hiking out on the windward rail when the boat is in a thirty-degree heel is quite a wild ride, and a wet one at that.

A news helicopter flew low overhead, the rotors thump-thump-thumping and drowning out the sound of the boat slicing through the flat water.

"It's nice to be famous," Chris said with a laugh.

We all watched the chopper circle us and then take off toward the rear of the fleet. We quickly began passing all the boats in our division as *Merlin* accelerated past Point Judith and left the land astern. Soon we caught up to the slower boats that had started earlier. We were even beating the catamarans, or gunboats. The 2018 Bermuda race marked the first time that multihulls were allowed to participate.

The boat settled in, making ten knots in 7.5 knots of wind. I could tell that my dad was impressed. He just couldn't stop smiling as we worked the boat as fast as we could in the light-air conditions, never letting up for a minute. The rest of the crew who were new to the boat were impressed too. I'd seen their eyes go wide during our only real practice session in a gusty fifteen- to twenty-two-knot westerly wind on Narragansett Bay under the full mainsail and a nonoverlapping jib.

In the gusts, the boat instantly accelerated and rapidly heeled over thirty degrees, burying the lee rail in the waves and sending sheets of spray flying aft. Whoops and hollers ensued as *Merlin* hit thirteen knots on a beam reach. Now that we were out in front of most of the fleet, even after such a terrible start, we wanted to keep our potentially winning position. We old-time Team *Merlin* vets had learned our lesson off Cuba, when we'd become complacent because we enjoyed such an extensive lead.

Chris Watts didn't have to repeat his playful gibe: "Gentlemen, are we racing or are we riding?" Even now, we talk about this a lot. On a long ocean race, crew motivation is essential. If the crew becomes lackadaisical or sloppy or if you, as the skipper, allow morale to sag when things aren't going your way, your team performance will suffer, and you'll probably lose the race. Lose a second here and there, and suddenly you've lost minutes. Seconds count in an ocean yacht race. Minutes are like entire days.

June in New England can get chilly. As the fleet heads to sea on a southwesterly breeze, the first night is typically cold. But if you're making good time, you'll be in the Gulf Stream at some point during the second day. The first hints of the tropics emerge in the form of puffy fair-weather cumulus clouds. As you get deeper into the Gulf Stream, the seas turn rough, and thunder squalls become common. The race usually takes three to six days, depending on the size of the boat.

The race is geared toward amateur sailors in "normal" boats, although the sleds with pro crews do show up. Race organizers put a solid emphasis on safety. In fact, several of the participants on each boat are required to take the US Sailing Safety at Sea course offered by the United States Sailing Association, commonly known as US Sailing. Brian and I had attended the US Sailing school in Annapolis before the race, and the experience was chilling. Knowing offshore ocean racing can be dangerous on an intellectual level is far less impressive than having the point driven home with figures to back up the instruction.

Part of the US Sailing Safety at Sea program involves lectures on what to do if someone falls overboard. On a racing boat doing twenty knots, the boat will be miles away from the person in the water before the crew can turn around and head back. One of the guest lecturers told a story about losing a crewman overboard during the Mackinac race on Lake Michigan. The Mackinac race was on the itinerary for 2018, so I naturally was interested in what the man was saying.

The incident he related occurred at night. While the crewman's personal flotation device, an auto-inflatable life jacket, was equipped with a light, it was impossible to distinguish it from the lights of the other boats. The waters of Lake Michigan are cold even in the summer, and as the minutes ticked on and the crew couldn't find the person in the water, hopes began to flag that the person would survive. Death by hypothermia was a distinct possibility. Finally, one of the people on the boat heard a high-pitched whistle. They found the person in the water because of the whistle, not the light. It was eye-opening to think that an old-fashioned whistle had saved a person's life.

After the Safety at Sea course, I was determined to beef up the safety aspects of the *Merlin* team. I felt that it was my responsibility as the owner and skipper of the yacht to do everything possible to protect the lives of my crew. We studied life jackets from a variety of manufacturers, and we found, to our surprise, that some tests revealed that the vest could actually push your face into the water when the device inflated.

We wanted vests that wouldn't inflate on deck if a wave washed over the bow, which happens all the time aboard *Merlin* because her freeboard is so low. For nonsailors, freeboard is the height of the hull from the waterline to the sheer line, or the top edge of where the hull meets the deck. On *Merlin*, the freeboard is just 4.15 feet forward, and only 3.25 feet aft. That means that a six-foot wave will be nearly three feet higher than the deck when you're sitting in the cockpit. A canoe has a freeboard of a bit more than a foot, which is saying something when you're comparing a fourteen-foot aluminum canoe to a seventy-one-foot racing sloop.

We settled on Mustang survival life jackets, and we upgraded the whistles to ones with a much higher pitch than those that normally came with the vests. We also bought the highest-quality foul-weather gear on the market to ensure that the crew would be comfortable and as dry as possible on our very wet boat.

As any sailor knows, however, the first order of business is to prevent being separated from the boat in the first place. This requires clipping onto a jack line, a flat, high-strength line that runs along the deck. We also rig jack lines in the cockpit because you can easily get swept overboard if the conditions are really rough.

The life jackets we bought were equipped with a harness. You attach a tether to the harness, and you use the carabiner at the other end of the tether to clip onto the jack line. If you need to move to another jack line, say up at the bow, then you use a second tether to clip on before you unclip the first tether. That way, you're always attached to the boat. It's a little like rock climbing. In either case, falling can be fatal.

While the Cuba and Mexico regattas were big events for me as a newbie to ocean racing, the Bermuda race was by far the biggest international regatta I'd ever sailed in. For me, it was a magical experience, especially since I was sharing it with my dad. I felt like I was part of something much larger than myself, and indeed I was. We all were. The sense of community, the conviviality, and the willingness to encourage and support each other even as we sought to beat every single competitor was something that I'd observed during my one-design racing days, but in these large ocean races there is a real difference in terms of emotional intensity. Perhaps that's because it's more possible to die on the ocean than it is in a bay or sound. Inshore and offshore can both be deadly. It's just that the ocean can be deadlier a lot faster, and you're pretty much on your own if things go south in a hurry.

The Newport-Bermuda race began in 1906, the same year the Transpacific Yacht Race from California to Hawaii got started. The East Coast regatta was the brainchild of Thomas Fleming Day, editor of *Rudder* magazine, a publication that targeted amateur sailors. Sailing was mostly a sport for the wealthy, but Day believed that promoting sailing through an international yacht race for smaller boats would benefit the sport as a whole, and his magazine in particular. The Industrial Revolution was in full swing, and the middle class was growing. If more people discovered sailing, that would benefit the recreational boating industry, which was in its infancy.

The Brooklyn Yacht Club (BYC) and the Royal Bermuda Yacht Club (RBYC) were the initial organizers. The race started in New York Harbor and ended near Saint David's Head in Bermuda. Only four other races were run after that, but the event was revived after World War I. In 1923, twenty-two boats entered the race, and apparently encountered rough seas and high winds. Three years later, the Cruising Club of America (CCA) teamed up with the RBYC to host the race together, and they've been doing it ever since.

In 1923, the commodore of the CCA, Herbert L. Stone, characterized the mission of the race as follows: "In order to encourage the designing, building, and sailing of small seaworthy yachts, to make popular cruising upon deep water, and to develop in the amateur sailor a love of true seamanship, and to give opportunity to become proficient in the art of navigation ..."

The race is often called "the thrash to the onion patch." When I first heard that expression, I was a bit confused. What did onions have to do with a yacht race? Then someone clued me in. The race is typically rough, most specifically in the Gulf Stream, and there are often high winds. Ocean sailors call this a "thrash," even if the wind is abeam or abaft the beam. The onion part is more of a mystery. I was told that Bermuda is sometimes referred to as the "onion patch" because of its agriculture. Only 20 percent of the land is arable, and the main crops include bananas, citrus fruits, vegetables, flowers, and honey. No onions. Go figure.

As it turned out, Day skippered the boat that won the first race in 1906, the thirty-eight-foot yawl *Tamerlane* owned by Franklin Maier. After completing the finish at Saint David's Head, Day picked up a tow for the journey of a couple hours into the port of Hamilton, Bermuda's capital. A crowd of about four thousand spectators greeted him with raucous cheers and applause. The entire population of the island at the time was just fourteen thousand. The race start was eventually moved to Newport, adding to that city's reputation as a premiere yachting center.

The rich history of the race made it even more special, at least to me, and standing at the helm out in front of most of the fleet made my day. I wondered if we were setting up for another stellar race, another like the one we'd just run from St. Petersburg, Florida, to Isla Mujeres, Mexico, in April.

On race day, April 26, we had gotten off to a great start, crossing the line almost at the gun, and proceeded to beat to windward, covering our archrival, *Sgt. Reckless*, a Tripp 75 that was favored to win. Everything I'd heard and read about *Merlin* indicated that she was not a great upwind performer, but as we eased under the Sunshine Skyway Bridge and left Tampa Bay behind us in about fifteen knots of wind, I was pleased to see that she was easily staying ahead of *Sgt. Reckless*.

The afternoon passed uneventfully, with *Sgt. Reckless* either dead even with us or slightly behind. She looked huge compared to the skinny *Merlin*, a veritable Goliath to our plucky David, even though she was only four feet longer overall.

Nothing motivates a racing sailor more than having a rival in plain sight. The crew hustled through sail changes, running up the "Rainbow Warrior," a giant A2 spinnaker adorned with a rainbow. The sail was in keeping with the theme of the boat's dark-blue paint job, with its distinctive rainbow that extended to the topsides and boom. Little white wizard stars speckled the blue background of the hull.

The sun went down and we lost sight of our rival, but we knew she was nearby. We set our course to the north to stay out of the worst currents, turning south once we got closer to Isla Mujeres. The tactic would add distance to our route, but we all believed we'd make more speed over ground to compensate for the additional distance.

I was at the helm when one of the crew came up from below. Based on the expression on his face, he was worried.

"The batteries are hot as hell," he said.

"How hot?" I asked.

"Real hot, man! Real hot!"

We'd installed a suite of batteries to power the sophisticated electronics we'd just purchased, and the batteries had grown so hot we thought they might catch on fire or explode. An electrical fire or an explosion are nightmares for anyone offshore in a boat. Choosing the prudent option, we shut down the bank of new electronics so that the batteries could cool. While we started tracking down the issue, we pulled out the trusty handheld backup GPS units. This after spending a fortune on state-of-the-art navigation gear! As they say, "Stuff happens." Stuff always happens on boats. About four hours later, we'd worked around the battery problem and had gotten the electronics going again.

As the second day and night passed, we pulled farther and farther ahead of the fleet, including *Sgt. Reckless*. At one point, we were about twenty miles ahead of the boat. The winds held fair and we kept sliding ahead. We knew we were on track to set a new course record, both for monohulls and multihulls.

When we got close enough to Isla Mujeres, we changed course to the south for a straight shot to the finish line. Our lead continued to lengthen, and as the sun came up, Mexico heaved into view. Then we saw the Mexican gunboat that was stationed at the finish line, and as we flew across at 08:59:00, I glanced toward the island and saw Donice waving from the point that flanks the entrance channel to the harbor. A one-person cheering squad, she was jumping up and down, waving, and cheering for us. She knows next to nothing about yacht racing, but Donice is *Merlin*'s most enthusiastic fan.

A small powerboat pulled up, its crew welcoming us with big smiles. As we followed our escort into the harbor, I wondered if we'd have enough water to actually get to the marina. I'd been told that the channel was only about ten or eleven feet deep, and *Merlin* draws eleven feet. She's definitely not designed for shallow harbors.

We got in just fine, but when we tried to leave several days later, we discovered that the keel had hollowed out a hole in the mud while the boat was at the dock. It was comical seeing the entire crew standing on the leeward side of the boat in an effort to tip her over enough to get out of the hole. On the first day, this trick did not work. On the next day at high tide, we powered out of the mud into open water.

The team was thrilled with the results of the race—mostly. We set a new course record with an elapsed time of one day, twenty-one hours, twenty-four minutes, and zero seconds, shaving seven hours off the monohull record and two hours off the multihull record. We were first to finish by a long way. And best of all, we finished two hours ahead of *Sgt. Reckless*. But when the corrected times were calculated based on the handicap rules, a boat that finished long after us won our class.

The Newport race, like other offshore races, is run on a handicap system. In theory, similar boats are rated together, evening out the competition within each class of boats. The formula is terribly complicated, and it's far too "in the weeds" for a discussion here. Suffice it to say that I was wondering how we could set a course record and still lose our class on corrected time. It's enough to give you a headache, but that's how it is in offshore ocean racing. The longer the race, the more challenge to the handicap, since boats across the racecourse will be experiencing different conditions. Indeed, many of the boats in the Mexico race stumbled into light air, and the fierce currents set them off course. Some boats finished days after we did.

My mind slowly returned from reminiscing about the Mexico race to focusing on the race at hand. The current conditions were not ideal to say the least. The sea heaved in low glassy swells. The boom swung back and forth, thumping the rig. The big main thundered when it lost air and flogged. Creaks, squeaks, clangs, and a million other boat sounds began to drive me crazy as we sat becalmed hundreds of miles out to sea. Any chance of setting a record, or even placing well in our division, seemed slim after the great first day en route to Bermuda.

I looked off to starboard. A big catamaran was our constant shadow, only a mile or so away.

I sighed and said, "Why don't we call those guys and see if they want to come over for some martinis? We could even go swimming."

"Yeah, we could have a real party," one of the crewmen said.

"Nothing else to do," another crewman said.

Like any sport, the mental aspect of sailboat racing is key. It's tough to keep everyone motivated to race when there's no wind and you're on deck baking in the sun. You just sit there looking at each other, hoping for a breeze and trying not to get on each other's nerves. It's easy to give in to the gloom and doom. It's also easy to lapse into negative self-talk that can infect everyone around you. By and large, the spirits of the crew were good, but the light air was definitely trying our collective patience.

"We're definitely in an eddy," the navigator piped up from the nav station below decks. "Looks like we're actually going backward."

Great, I thought, *just what the doctor ordered. A flat calm in the middle of the ocean.*

The news got worse when we checked the tracker app on the computer. The fleet was spread out, but the smaller boats we'd passed on the first day were creeping up because the wind was filling in from behind us. Big boats like us were caught in an area of bad air.

> Life is full of things we can't control. The question is how you react to a situation you can't change, and you do have a choice in that.

The frustration aboard was palpable, but Dad, always quick with a joke, kept us all smiling as he quipped about this and that. He even broke out into a sea shanty or two. He kept us smiling despite the circumstances.

If there's nothing you can do about something, you just have to accept it. Life is full of things we can't control. The question is how you react to a situation you can't change, and you do have a choice in that. I had to consciously make an effort to drive negativity away, both for me and the crew. I knew the wind would come up eventually, and it did.

Sunday was Father's Day, and we ushered it in while ghosting along with a staysail and main. The big cat was still with us, and I figured she probably would be for the duration of the race.

"What the heck is that?" one of the watch crew said. He pointed at a dark rectangular object awash about twenty-five yards off the starboard bow. Everyone came on deck to look at it.

"Shipping container," Brian announced.

"God," I said, "can you imagine hitting that at twenty miles an hour in the middle of the night?"

We all agreed that we didn't want to think about the consequences of a collision with a massive steel shipping container. I'd seen containers on ships before, and I was vaguely aware that these containers are sometimes swept off the decks during bad storms. Most containers sink. But some stay afloat for months or even longer, with just the top of the container visible to a sharp-eyed lookout. The things are like submarine icebergs, or mines ready to shatter the hull in an instant after an explosive impact.

At one of the prerace meetings, a race official had asked us to keep an eye out for balloons, and to count any we saw. As with the containers, I was vaguely aware that helium balloons can escape, fly over the ocean, and drop to the surface while remaining partially inflated. These balloons pose a significant threat to whales, sharks, sea turtles, seals, walruses, and other marine life that mistake them for food. We saw hundreds of balloons on the way to Bermuda, and it saddened all of us to see how much pollution was floating around out there.

Plastics in the oceans represent a major problem, and balloons are just a small part of the bigger picture. Plastic bags, water bottles, bottle caps, Styrofoam cups, fishing nets, and other debris litter the oceans. Beaches on the windward side of remote tropical islands are often choked with plastic debris.

The biggest example of an oceanic plastic dump is known as the Great Pacific Garbage Patch, an area south of Hawaii that measures 1.6 million square miles. It's composed of trillions of tiny bits of plastic (microplastics) that have been broken down by the sun and the motion of the sea. The microplastics float on or just under the surface until they finally sink, and they pose the same threat to marine life as the bigger plastic debris does. Circular ocean currents in the Pacific draw the microplastics into a vortex that traps them in the center. Think of it as a giant whirlpool of tiny plastic nuggets. A sort of soup made of indigestible garbage.

Scientists did not discover the Great Pacific Garbage Patch. That honor went to a yacht-racing skipper named Charles Moore. In 1997, Moore participated in the Transpac from California to Hawaii, the same year that *Pyewacket* broke *Merlin*'s 1977 record. On his way back from the race, he crossed the North Pacific Tropical Gyre and found he'd entered an area of ocean filled with plastics of all sorts. The microplastics gave the ocean a soupy appearance. Later studies concluded that there are 1.9 million bits of plastic per square mile. The microplastics don't decompose much further before eventually sinking to the bottom of the ocean. Some scientists believe that the ocean floor of the patch is nothing more than a thick carpet of microplastics.

The sight of all that plastic induced Moore to found the Algalita Marine Research Foundation to raise awareness of plastic pollution in the oceans, and to study the Great Pacific Garbage Patch. In 2014, he led an expedition to the patch, where he used drones to fly over a large area, and the drones discovered plastic islands more than fifty feet long floating in the microplastics stew. His group concluded that the patch contained one hundred times more plastics by weight than previously estimated.

In another quirky yachting angle, sailor, explorer, and ecologist David de Rothschild dreamed up the crazy idea of building a sixty-foot catamaran from plastic bottles to raise awareness of the plastic-pollution problem. Essentially, the team at Adventure Ecology used thousands of reclaimed plastic bottles in place of fiberglass, melting them down and using them to lay up the mold. The scheme worked. The team named the catamaran *Plastiki*, a play on Thor Heyerdahl's *Kon-Tiki* raft, which he famously sailed across the Pacific Ocean in 1947. In 2010, the Adventure Ecology crew successfully sailed *Plastiki* from San Francisco, California, to Sydney, Australia.

I had never been active in any marine-conservation movements. The issues were just not on my radar screen, but they are now. One of the things I want to do with *Merlin* is to use her to promote safe sailing, and to raise awareness about the importance of addressing the ocean-pollution problem. Seeing all those balloons really did it for me. Sometimes, I guess you've got to actually see to believe.

I saw. I now believe.

The Monday after Father's Day brought more slow sailing, and yet we never let up on trying to get the most speed out of the boat. We were falling behind other yachts in our division, based on corrected time. We were physically the leader of our division in terms of position, but the handicap rules were doing us in. Tuesday dawned fair, hot, and calm. Slowly, we crawled, banged, clanged, and flapped our way to Bermuda.

The island first appeared as a faint smudge on the horizon, the lush green of the hilltops growing more distinct as time passed. Suddenly I felt a puff, and I saw ripples spread across the low groundswell. I could've done the dance of joy. As it was, I beamed at the crew and said, "Let's get going, guys! We've got a race to win!" Dad just grinned at me.

And the wind did fill in at around 3:30 p.m., enough so we could really sail *Merlin* at last. We made good time tacking along the shore of Saint David's Island. Bermuda, despite the singular name, is a collection of islands surrounded by treacherous reefs. I thought of the many warnings we'd received about navigating the waters near Saint

David's Head Light, a lighthouse built atop the cliffs on the northeast side of Saint David's Island.

"Whatever you do, stay in the channel!" we were told. "Reefs can be very unforgiving."

The crew was all business as we tacked closer and closer to the finish line. The sea was an aquamarine expanse dappled with the shimmering sparkle of the sun. On the grounds above the cliffs, we saw multicolored houses with red-tiled roofs. The breeze carried the scent of oleander. The scene was something right out of a storybook.

"God, it's beautiful," I said to Dad, who was perched next to me by the helm. "Now I know why you loved talking about the Bermuda race so much!"

"Never gets old," he said with a huge smile.

"Mr. Bill Merlin!" I said, gesturing to the helm, "take her on in!"

"Sure thing," he said, emotion roughening his voice. He took the helm, skippering the boat through a few more tacks. Closer, closer, closer …

The radio hissed, and a voice with a British accent said, "Congratulations, yacht *Merlin*! You've finished the race!"

"Roger that," the person on our radio replied. "Thanks. We can't wait to get into Hamilton."

"The party's already started."

I bet it has, I thought.

"We'll be there for some rum punch in about two hours. Sailing vessel *Merlin* out."

The exchange had taken less than a minute as the crew of *Merlin* cheered, slapped backs, fist bumped, and jumped up and down. I hugged my dad, stepped back, and simply drank in the moment. All fourteen of us tough, weather-beaten sailors choked up. We all knew that this race was the impetus for buying *Merlin*, that the crossing was a gift to my dad.

It was getting late, so we put the celebrating on hold until we reached Hamilton. We doused the sails, turned on the motor, and headed into port. We finished the race at about four p.m., or officially at 16:11:52, on June 19. Our elapsed time of ninety-seven hours, forty-one minutes, and fifty-two seconds gave us a first-to-finish position in our division, but on corrected time we placed eighth, or dead last.

To give you an idea of how slow the passage was, compare it to the record for the fastest race that was set in 2016 when the one-hundred-foot maxi yacht *Comanche* made it in an astounding thirty-four hours, forty-two minutes, and fifty-three seconds, at an average speed of 18.3 knots. A day and a half, compared to our four-plus days!

As we entered the harbor, I turned to Dad and said, "Well, does it look the same as it did in 1956?"

He gave me a wry smile. "Not really. But you know, everything changes."

He was right about that. I considered all that had happened in just over a year. I'd gone on a lark race with my friend Dave Kilcoyne in 2017, and bam! I was the proud owner of *Merlin*, and I'd just sailed her in the Newport-Bermuda race with my dad.

Ain't life grand?

7

MACKINAC

I AWOKE FULL OF anticipation on Saturday, July 21, 2018. In the dim light of dawn, I could see that the day was overcast as I stared out the window of the Airbnb my crew and I were staying in. The sky over Lake Michigan was gunmetal gray, with darker scud moving fast. I checked the latest weather report and noted that the wind was predicted to be out of the north at twenty to twenty-five knots, with six- to eight-foot seas.

At least we won't be stuck in a light-air race, I thought.

Within days of completing the Newport-Bermuda race, a delivery crew had sailed *Merlin* back to Newport, where she was loaded onto a truck for transport to Chicago. The next race on our schedule was already here: the 110th Chicago Yacht Club Race to Mackinac.

First run in 1898, the Mac is a 333-mile thrash north up the length of Lake Michigan to Mackinac Island, a tiny dot of 3.8 square miles on Lake Huron at the eastern end of the Straits of Mackinac. It's the longest annual freshwater race in the world, and it's known for its unpredictable conditions. Weather systems blow in from the west, churning Lake Michigan into a boiling cauldron of steep waves with short periods, meaning there isn't much distance between crest and trough, unlike the long rollers you get in midocean.

When the wind drives in from the north on Lake Michigan, you've got a "fetch" of hundreds of miles for the waves to build before they pile up on the south shore at Chicago. Fetch is the distance of open water a wave has to build up on. The shorter the fetch, the smaller the wave. The precise opposite occurs when you have a long fetch. In the Southern Ocean, you have unlimited fetch, which is why the waves are so big down there all the time. There's nothing to break them up.

The Mac was born out of a rivalry between the owners of two sloops designed by Joseph Myers: the fifty-nine-foot *Siren* and the sixty-four-foot *Vanenna*. Built at the Racine Boat Manufacturing Company in 1886, both boats had fin keels and were notoriously fast. The owners of the yachts—George Peate of *Siren*, and W. R. Crawford of *Vanenna*—first faced off in two inconclusive races.

In 1898, members of the Chicago Yacht Club dreamed up an idea for a long-distance race to fan interest in sailing, and to drum up more members for the club. They chose Mackinac Island as the finish for what became the Mac, in part because many of the members had summer vacation homes on the island.

Known to Native Americans as the "place of the great turtle" because of its turtle-like shape, the island was once a key commercial center for the fur trade. By the 1890s, it had firmly established itself as a playground for the wealthy. It's still a popular resort town.

That first Mac featured the two sloops, *Siren* and *Vanenna*, and three schooners. Peate and Crawford battled it out for most of the race, but *Vanenna* won with an elapsed time of fifty-two hours, seventeen minutes, and fifty seconds. *Siren* finished second in the race, coming in thirty-seven minutes and twenty seconds behind *Vanenna*.

As hoped, interest in the race helped boost the membership of the Chicago Yacht Club. The race has been an annual event since 1921.

In 1998, Steve Fossett scorched the previous multihull record with a staggering run of just eighteen hours and fifty minutes with the big cat *Stars and Stripes*. Roy E. Disney's *Pyewacket* set the monohull record in 2002 with a passage of twenty-three hours, thirty minutes.

Naturally, I hoped to beat *Pyewacket*'s time, and I figured that might be possible, given the forecast. We'd often sailed *Merlin* upwind, but never in conditions like the ones we were expecting on the race-course. Unless the wind shifted, it would be a hard beat to windward the whole way. I wondered how the boat would perform. She wasn't designed for what we were asking her to do.

As I got dressed. I heard other members of the crew stirring. The murmur of quiet conversation was coming from the kitchen. Like me, everyone else was keyed up and ready for the race. I knew it would be rough out there. I just didn't know how bad it would get.

Lake Michigan deserves respect. Severe thunder squalls are common. Sustained gale-force winds battered the fleets in 1911, 1937, and 1970, but there were no fatalities in the race until July 17, 2011. A bit before midnight, a violent thunderstorm sprang up off Fox Island, about thirteen miles northwest of Charlevoix, Michigan. The thirty-five-foot *WingNuts* was sailing fast. All eight crew members were harnessed in and wearing life jackets when the squall hit.

In a matter of seconds, the yacht capsized in wind gusts that exceeded seventy miles per hour. Mark Morley, age fifty-one and a veteran of twenty Mackinac races, and Suzanne Bickel, age forty-one, both suffered massive blunt-force head trauma as the boat turned upside down, the mast pointing toward the bottom of the lake. Still attached to their tethers, both sailors drowned under the boat. The six other members of the crew were rescued within about fifteen minutes, but it was too late for Morley and Bickel.

Some reports filed after the accident indicated that the radical racing design of the Kiwi 35 wasn't suited for offshore racing. So, was the accident a freak? A fluke? Or did the sailors tempt fate by running an ultralight displacement boat like her in an offshore race on a lake that can sink big ships? Who can say? Certainly, Bill Lee received his share of similar naysaying about light boats and high seas. As noted, he believed light was better in storms because the boat gives instead of pounding into the waves. But sometimes even a Ping-Pong ball can get crushed. Mother Nature is just that powerful.

The Chicago skyline looked foreboding as we guided *Merlin* out of her slip. Once we got into the lake proper—the start is located off the Chicago Lighthouse, near the Navy Pier—the boat began to buck and pitch. When sailing to windward, she dipped her bow deep in the troughs and rocketed the stern up high on the crests. It felt like riding one of those electric bucking broncos you sometimes find in country and western bars. Cold spray flew all the way back to the stern. The crew hiking out on the windward rail turned their faces aft to avoid the worst of it.

In conditions like these, you tether yourself to the boat, and you hold on tight for dear life. You watch every step, and you secure a handhold before you move. The violent motion of the boat was enough to throw you overboard or send you smashing into a bulkhead below if you weren't holding on. The "sweet water," which is what saltwater folks call the Great Lakes, was showing its gnarly side.

Trying to stay in clear air and not hit another competitor, I steered us into the parade of boats bound for the Navy Pier. I heard the announcer telling the thousands of spectators a little about each boat as the crews sailed past the pier. I couldn't help but smile when it was our turn to enjoy the pageantry. We waved to the crowd, cheered, and joked. Then we sailed into the confusion of sleek hulls, tall masts, and colorful sails as we waited to start. As usual, the smaller boats started first. We had some time to kill, and I figured we'd sail downwind just to see what *Merlin* would do in those conditions.

When we were ready, up went the chute. The big spinnaker filled immediately, and I felt *Merlin* accelerate as if I'd shot her out of a cannon. The wheel vibrated. The rigging hummed. Every part of the boat was in tune with the wind and water. Suddenly, she squatted down in the stern, and the bow went up. We left a prodigious rooster tail in our wake, and white water blasted off the hull as she surged on like a torpedo.

"Holy cow!" I yelled, briefly glancing aft at our wake. "She's on plane!"

Chris shot me a look that said, "This is the fastest you've had *Merlin* flying, and the race hasn't even started!"

The entire crew whooped, shouted, and gave the thumbs-up as *Merlin*'s speed exceeded twenty knots. We'd never gotten her up on plane before, mainly because most of our previous races were in light air, and partly because the boat was still so new to us all. Even though we were late into the 2018 racing season and had gotten to know the boat, we were still on a steep learning curve. We'd only had one day to practice before the Mac.

It seemed like we were always pushing the envelope on time. Maybe that was my fault. Maybe I tried to cram as much racing as possible into the season because I was overly enthusiastic. Boat upgrades delayed us for the Cuba race and for the Bermuda race, limiting our practice time. So, was it the fault of the boatyards that we didn't have time to practice enough before the races?

It's easy to blame others when things don't go exactly as planned, and I try not to do that. I take responsibility for our rushed practice sessions. The boatyards played a part, but the buck stops with the skipper and owner. The buck stops on the desk of the CEO as well. I was aware, painfully aware, that I hadn't built in enough time to hone the skills of the crew as a collective unit.

Each member of the crew had fabulous skills as an individual sailor. That's not enough, though. You have to have each sailor complementing the skills of his or her teammates. Everyone needs to know each other well enough to communicate almost without words. One reason I rented the Airbnb was to bring the crew together under one roof, thereby setting up the right situation for the team to actually become a team instead of an assortment of individual parts. I really like being with the crew and discussing the thousand and one little things we can do to be better and faster. Still, we should have had more practice time. None of us knew much about sweet-water sailing. I know I certainly didn't.

Chris flashed me a smile. "Pretty amazing, isn't she."

"And how!" I said, grinning from ear to ear. Running the Mac was a milestone moment for me and the boat. It was an iconic race, fitting of her pedigree. And now we'd sailed the boat faster than we had ever sailed her before. Another milestone moment.

"Three minutes to start," Brian said.

We prepared sail settings for upwind performance north to Mackinac Island and jockeyed for the best position at the starting line. Boats tacked back and forth all around us. We couldn't stay in clear air. The sails of the other boats blanketed us or left us in the disturbed air aft of the boats. We crossed the line late and continued fighting to get free of the throng, tacking between two boats to find the slot we were looking for to get us into clear air. We quickly began catching up with the smaller boats that had left before us.

The waves were short and steep as we sailed to windward. Sheets of spray flew aft, showering the crew as they sat decked out in full foul-weather gear and inflatable Mustang life jackets. Any spare hands were hiked out on the windward rail to keep the boat sailing as flat as possible. *Merlin* sailed with the lee rail under most of the time anyway, with about thirty degrees of heel. It was difficult to move around without getting thrown into a winch. In fact, my side ached from a crash into the cockpit coaming when the boat suddenly lurched and I lost my balance, coming down hard on my ribs. Something didn't feel right to me about the way *Merlin* was handling. It seemed like I was doing something wrong, and I wasn't sure of what. I felt the boat shaking and vibrating like she never had before.

Putting ego aside after about fifteen minutes into the race, I said to Chris, "I'm just not hitting it right. Let's switch. You take the helm for about forty-five minutes, and I'll play the main."

As we switched places, I told him I wanted to watch his technique to learn how to sail the boat to windward in conditions like these. Of all the people aboard, he had the most experience sailing the boat. I noticed he had a subtle hand on the helm, and that he got into a rhythm, easing her off the backs of the waves into the troughs, and then up the next wave. We weren't sailing in a straight line; rather, we were weaving through the valleys and avoiding the mountaintops as much as we could. The shaking and vibrations didn't stop, but I felt like she'd fallen into the groove on the port tack after Chris took over. Our speed definitely picked up in the northeasterly winds, which were now gusting at over twenty-five knots.

About twenty-five minutes after the start, we caught one of the smaller boats, *Imedi*, a TP52 that was racing in the "Turbo" section.

The fifty-two-footer was sailing fast to weather of us, and, as we passed her, she fell off to leeward into the eddies and whirls of disturbed air that had just come off our massive sails.

"That boat's acting really weird," I said, pointing. "Look! She's heading up into the wind! What the hell is going on?"

Then I watched in confusion as *Imedi* fell off the wind and began to turn around. I looked over at Brian and saw his face was grim.

"Someone fell overboard," he said. "We should get ready to go back. Do we have a man-overboard signal?" he shouted to the navigator, who was down below. The urgency in his voice was obvious.

"No!"

Now *Imedi* sailed downwind. Something bad was happening.

Brian turned to me and said, "Let's go back. There's something wrong. I—"

"Man overboard! Man overboard on *Imedi*!" the navigator shouted. "We just got the alert!"

Brian instantly shouted to the pit crew, "We're turning back!"

Chris carefully and deliberately turned us around, easing the boat off the wind for our run back to *Imedi*. I couldn't help but imagine how the people aboard the yacht were feeling. I imagined the panic and having to fight against it. I imagined the crew throwing everything that floated overboard for the lost sailor to find. I looked out at the waves and pictured myself in the water, surging to the top of a crest, where I could see all the boats sailing around me, and then sliding into the trough, where I could see nothing but dark water.

The water temperature was around seventy degrees Fahrenheit, which wasn't terribly cold but was still dangerous if you were immersed for a long time. Water conducts heat twenty-five times more efficiently than air, which means you lose more heat when you're swimming than if you're caught in the cold on top of a mountain. Both scenarios can kill you. It's just that cold water will most likely kill you faster. The sailor probably had about an hour or two to live before hypothermia set in, causing heart and respiratory failure, so time was of the essence. We all assumed that the sailor's life jacket had inflated. All we had to do was find the person before he or she died from hypothermia.

In about five minutes or so (the official report says it took us longer to get back), we were abreast of *Imedi* and sailing farther downwind to see if we could find the missing sailor. Seven other boats broke off from the race to help the coast guard and police with the search as well. The race participants were first on the scene, though. We started sailing in ever-widening circles under a reefed main and jib. We were no longer racing. We had to go slowly enough so that all spare hands could keep a weather eye out for the sailor in the water.

"I see something!" shouted one of the crew, pointing at what looked like just a bunch of waves to me. "Over there!"

Then I saw it too. Something yellow. Something floating. My heart raced with joy. We'd found the missing sailor. We got closer, closer …

"Damn it!" I shouted. "It's a damned horseshoe buoy."

The joy of moments before vanished. Little else was said. We continued the search. Later, the same scenario played out when we found an orange balloon floating in the water. It's difficult to describe the emotions everyone felt, particularly when we thought we'd found the missing sailor twice. Hours passed, and still the missing sailor hadn't been found.

It became clear to everyone that we were no longer looking for a living human being; we were looking for a corpse. I still get choked up about it, and I was close to tears during the search as we somberly sailed, the wind moaning in the rigging, the waves washing in as always. The lake had taken another soul to its dark, cold bosom. The power of nature is indifferent to the ways of humankind, and we'd just been given a painful reminder of just how small an individual person is in comparison to the universe.

At about five o'clock, roughly four hours after the accident, Brian said, "Okay, we can't find him. Should we get back into the race?"

I thought about it. Most of the boats in our division were way out ahead of us. And besides, I didn't have any desire to race after what had happened. A person had most probably died in what was supposed to be a fun event. While I knew intellectually that offshore sailboat racing was inherently dangerous, it was another matter entirely to actually participate in a search-and-rescue operation that had apparently failed.

"To be honest with you, Brian, I think I'd like to head back to the yacht club and get a stiff drink," I said. "I don't feel like racing."

Everyone agreed. The race was over for us. With heavy hearts, we sailed back to our slip, the skyline of Chicago as gray and gloomy as ever in the late-afternoon light. Somewhere out on the lake, the sleek S&S 50 *Challenge* was at the front of the fleet. She would ultimately land in the winner's circle, winning the race on an elapsed time of fifty-five hours, four minutes, and forty-eight seconds.

We later learned that the lost sailor, Jon Santarelli, age fifty-three, was going aft to trim the sails when a wave washed him under the lifelines in the cockpit. He drowned because his life jacket didn't inflate. The crew reported seeing him slip beneath the waves, a sight that will no doubt haunt all aboard for the rest of their lives. His body wasn't recovered until July 28.

One more tragedy occurred when Santarelli's family incinerated his life jacket along with his body during the cremation. Evidently, there was some kind of mix-up. The life jacket was vital evidence for the accident report. Now no one will ever know why the life jacket didn't inflate because no investigation could be done.

Santarelli's death really threw me, and I declined to join the celebrations held on Mackinac Island after the race. In the coming days, I thought about why people pursue dangerous sports like rock climbing, race car driving, white-water rafting, skydiving, and other activities that can get you killed. I wondered why I did. One-design racing can be hazardous, but it's usually pretty tame. There's not a lot of risk in it.

Offshore sailboat racing is dangerous. It's risky business. If I am honest with myself, I have to admit that part of the thrill of racing *Merlin* is overcoming whatever Mother Nature throws at us. Every time we race, we will either win or lose, and every time we race, we know we're pushing the limits of safety as we try to coax as much speed out of the boat as possible, sometimes under adverse conditions, like the ones we had at the start of the Mac. The adrenaline rush when *Merlin* goes up on plane is like no other, and it can bewitch you. The sea, for all her indifferent power, can cast a magic spell on you, luring you back time after time.

Life is short. Life is fragile. And life should be lived to the fullest. Santarelli's death drove that home in stark terms. We don't know how much time we have left. We just have today, and so we'd better make the most of it, since tomorrow may not come. I relish a quote by Mark Twain: "Twenty years from now you will be more disappointed by the things you didn't do than by the ones you did do." So, cast off your lines. Sail away from the safe harbor. Catch the trade winds in your sails. Explore! Dream! Discover!

It's easy to make excuses for not taking time to lead a full life, and many people do just that. They put off until tomorrow what they could (and should) do today. That's why I try to find a balance between my work and personal lives. It would be easy to work all the time, thereby ignoring the people around me, but then I would only be half a man. I wouldn't have the fullness of love, friendship, and shared experiences that complete a person emotionally and psychologically. For me, I find it's best to actually write personal goals down, and then to keep track of whether I've achieved the goal, how far I have to go to make it happen, and what is getting in the way if I'm having trouble moving ahead.

> You wouldn't sail a boat to Bermuda without charts. Why would you sail forth in the only life you've got to live without knowing where you want to go?

Businesses and other organizations write action plans all the time, but not many of us write down what we want in our personal lives and then take active steps to make it happen. Think about it. You wouldn't sail a boat to Bermuda without charts. Why would you sail forth in the only life you've got to live without knowing where you want to go?

Getting back into sailing was important to me. I added that to my life list during the 2017 Cuba race while chatting with Brian about big-boat ocean racing. And then I went for it, joining the St. Petersburg Yacht Club, buying *Mad Cow* without even sailing her first, and joining the Davis Island Yacht Club. Then I serendipitously ended up buying *Merlin* from Bill Lee. Thus far, I've done everything I set out to do with *Merlin*. Having accomplished what I wanted to do gives me immense satisfaction, and that is just one of many rewards that come when you actively live the life you want to live.

When bad things happen, you've got two choices. You can let it get you down, or you can pick yourself up and keep on going. The tragic death of Jon Santarelli certainly did put a damper on our experiences in Chicago, but we didn't let it stop us from carrying on with our plans to compete in the twenty-sixth running of the annual Verve Cup Offshore Regatta.

Hosted by the Chicago Yacht Club in August, this race was more like the one-design regattas of my past. Rather than a long point-to-point race, the racecourse takes you upwind for about two miles and then back dead downwind for two miles. Each race covers about eight miles, in four legs. Triangular courses are run as well. With the regatta in mind, Brian recruited additional professional sailors to join the crew in what turned out to be an exciting series of races that also provided us with a good education in terms of how to sail the boat at maximum efficiency.

We had plenty to learn about *Merlin*, and I relied on the professionals to show me the ropes in a competitive setting. We were by far the biggest and fastest boat in the fleet of 102 yachts at the regatta, which meant we'd be giving back a lot of time to the eight boats in our division based on the handicap rating. I knew these races would be won or lost in seconds, not minutes, and that we would have to drive the boat as hard as possible to avoid losing on corrected time.

The first race day dawned warm, bright, and sunny with a light wind of ten knots. As we tacked back and forth at the start, I gazed at the Chicago skyline, the buildings shimmering in the light, the lake a shade of deep blue. The contrast between this day and the start of the Mac couldn't have been more pronounced. The three fleets gathered at the line, and as usual, the smallest boats started first.

We made a good start, pointing high and fine on the rhumb line. The boat matched or exceeded the wind speed on the upwind leg, and we quickly began passing through the two fleets of smaller boats. In one or two tacks, we made the mark. We had eighteen crew members aboard, and each position worked like that proverbial well-oiled machine. We rounded the mark for the downwind blast, and controlled chaos ensued. As the jib came down, the Rainbow Warrior went up, filling in behind the main and easing out enough to create a lee while the spinnaker was raised and poled out.

Merlin took off. In what seemed like a blink of an eye, we were back down to the mark and ready to go upwind again. I recalled what Chris had said during the Cuba race: "Gentlemen, are we racing or are we riding?"

In a regatta like the Verve Cup, you can't let your guard down for a moment. Every second counts. Sail changes have to go fast and flawlessly. Indeed, in a race like this one, sail-handling skill is of paramount importance. In previous races, we didn't have to do anywhere near as many sail changes in so little time. I was on the helm during the entire series, and I believe I learned a lot about the boat in sailing a race that was quite similar to a one-design regatta. And I'd been right. We won and lost races by mere seconds.

At the end of the series, *Merlin* was in the lead, but only by a sliver. Any mistakes could have cost us the win. Ultimately, we won our division by a total of seven seconds on corrected time. The triumph was a good way to end what had been an emotional stay in Chicago, and it was a solid finish to close out the 2018 racing season.

All in all, we hadn't done badly, especially given the steep learning curve we were on. We won first-to-finish and line honors in the Cuba race. We set a course record and were the first boat to finish in the Mexico race. We bombed in the Bermuda race, but that adventure with my dad was special. Mackinac needs no further mention, and finally, we won our division in the Verve Cup.

The Verve Cup marked a milestone for *Merlin*. At the end of the racing season, our crew broke her down for the truck that would take her to Long Beach, California, where she'd undergo a major retrofit to get her ready to compete in the fiftieth Transpacific Yacht Race in

July 2019. She would no longer sport the bright-blue, star-spangled hull with the rainbow extending up to the boom. She would get a new paint job that would revert her looks back to the original white hull, with *Merlin* painted in big red letters on each side. She would get a new mast, boom, and traveler system.

In short, a swarm of skilled craftsmen were about to descend on the boat, with the sole objective of making her safer and easier to sail fast. *Merlin* would, in a real sense, morph into a new version of her old self, which seemed quite fitting for a boat named after a wizard.

8

RETROFIT

BRIGHT FLUORESCENT LAMPS lit the interior of the cavernous warehouse at Diversified Composites, the boatbuilding company I'd selected to undertake *Merlin*'s major retrofit. It was December 2018, and I'd flown to Long Beach to meet with the company's president, Dennis Choate, to finalize the project action plan. I stood in front of *Merlin*, and I found myself slightly in awe of how dismantled she looked.

I was used to seeing her in full racing mode, complete with the Rainbow Warrior flying and drawing fair. Seeing her propped upright in jack stands in the middle of a work area alive with activity was something altogether different. Workers swarmed over the boat as if she were being boarded by a band of pirates brandishing odd weapons.

Merlin has had nine owners, including Bill Lee and me. While most left the boat as she was originally designed, some modifications have occurred over the years. For example, *Merlin* was originally 66.5 feet long, but a "sugar-scoop stern" added in the 1980s extended her length to 68.5 feet and opened up the aft end of the boat. What is a sugar-scoop stern? Picture the back of a sailboat. The back end can go straight up and down perpendicular to the water, or it can angle inward, leaving an overhang. With the scoop, the stern angle is reversed outward, and the design typically features an open back, usually accommodating swim steps. If you've seen bikini-clad models in yachting magazines, then you've probably also seen a sugar-scoop stern. The easy access to the cockpit makes this style of stern popular in charter-boat designs.

The biggest change to the boat over the years involved the installation of a canting keel. A canting, or moveable, keel represents an example of how offshore racing sailboats have evolved over time. As boats went to the ultralight design Bill Lee pioneered, the problem of excessive heel when sailing to weather became obvious. The boats would sail on their sides more often than on the keel. That may be a bit of an exaggeration, but you get the idea. With her narrow beam and ultralight displacement, *Merlin* was the epitome of tender, meaning she liked to sail on her sides. The big sails frequently overpowered her, even in relatively light air when sailing close-hauled. Of course, she liked to submarine when sailing downwind.

Basically, a canting keel is comprised of a long skinny strut that extends below the hull of the boat, like an ordinary fixed keel. A bulb that looks an awful lot like a torpedo is attached to the bottom of the strut to act as ballast. When the boat starts to heel, the crew uses a mechanism inside the cabin that cranks the canting keel to the windward side of the boat, thereby greatly counteracting the force of the wind on the sails.

Being able to adjust the ballast position for better trim translates into faster speeds in the modern sled classes. Racing yacht designs began to evolve around the canting-keel concept, and soon more and more wide boats with canting keels were competing in major offshore yacht races. Nowadays, that's pretty much all you see.

In the 1990s, a previous owner installed a canting keel on *Merlin*. We believe he did so to get better windward performance out of the yacht, and to make her more competitive in the modern offshore racing fleet. When he told Bill Lee what he was preparing to do, Bill warned him that a canting keel wouldn't work well on *Merlin*. Bill designed *Merlin* in part based on the concept of a narrow Hawaiian sailing canoe, with one or two outriggers for stability. A long deep ballasted keel eliminated the need for outriggers, but the boat still wasn't meant to race upwind. Hawaiian sailing canoes weren't either. The light displacement and relatively little wetted surface meant she wouldn't track as well as boats with heavier displacement and more wetted surface on the keel.

The retrofit for the canting keel had been quite involved. Obviously, the fixed keel had to be removed. Not so obvious was the need to raise the cabin height to accommodate the movement mechanism. The extra weight of the gear contributed to the boat's poor performance with the device. The one benefit was that the boat stayed a little drier, because the water sloshing aft down the deck every time the bow plunged had to travel higher to go over the top of the cabin before it poured into the cockpit like a river. You still had to securely close the companionway to avoid filling the bilges, but she was less wet in a seaway. The downside of the higher cabin was that it made walking fore and aft on deck more difficult.

When Bill Lee was readying *Merlin* for the 2017 Transpac, one of the first things he did was to get rid of the canting keel. He hired yacht designer Alan Andrews to design a new and more efficient keel better suited to *Merlin*'s hull design. The keel that came off the drawing boards was deeper than the original, at eleven feet. Half the weight of the boat, 12,000 pounds, was in the bulb, or torpedo. The keel was also thinner, almost like the strut on a canting keel.

A couple of other changes were made. In 2004, a new carbon fiber mast was installed. The owner also had the boat painted in the rainbow theme. The bowsprit was added around 2010 to provide additional flexibility in sail sets. The sprit added 2.4 feet, bringing her total sparred length to seventy-one feet. All these modifications would pale next to the ones we now had planned for *Merlin*.

> Nothing remains stagnant, and racing yacht design is no exception. In many ways, it's the same in business.

If we expected to win, then we had to make some changes for the better. Nothing remains stagnant, and racing yacht design is no exception. In many ways, it's the same in business. If you're afraid to make necessary capital improvements to stay current with your competitors, then you can't expect to win the race to the top of your industry. Constant innovation and continual improvements to personnel and facilities are essential for keeping a competitive edge. If you're making positive moves to improve the company and the team, then you're being responsive to market trends and changes in technology.

On board *Merlin*, if I didn't act to correct obvious deficiencies that had developed over time as her more modern competitors had evolved (from a design standpoint), then how could I expect to win races against some of the most talented teams in the world? How could I expect *Merlin* to stand a chance of winning the Transpac in 2019, something I very much wanted to do?

So, as we all stood in the warehouse looking at *Merlin*, I suspected that I was in for an interesting afternoon as we went over the action plan with Dennis Choate. The fun started right away with the hole saw.

"Well, before we go much further with this job, we need to test the integrity of the hull," Dennis said. "I want to make sure we don't have wet core."

Balsa core sandwiched between two thin layers of fiberglass makes for a strong and light build, but there is always the risk of water ingress into the balsa through microcracks in the gelcoat. Water seeps into the balsa and migrates outward from the crack, greatly weakening the structural integrity of the hull. Wet core is a common problem with balsa-core builds, especially in older boats exposed to the rigors of ocean racing.

"What's that thing for?" I asked, nodding toward the hole saw Dennis was holding.

"I don't want you to freak out, Chip," Dennis said, "but we got to drill into her to take some core samples."

I was vaguely reminded of a geology class I took when I was an undergraduate at the University of Florida. I'd learned that geologists sometimes drill deep into rock to get a look at the sedimentary layers, but I wasn't so sure I liked the idea of drilling holes in my boat. "Core samples?" I asked, feeling a little confused and nervous.

Dennis nodded. "Yeah. Core samples. We gotta get 'em. We do use moisture meters to identify wet core, but there's nothing like taking a physical sample to eyeball up close and personal."

"Okay, let's go for it," I said, the hesitation clear in my voice.

Brian Malone, who was with me on this important trip, just shook his head and grinned. "It'll be fine. Yards do this all the time," Brian said.

I had to trust in the experts. I knew I'd be adrift without them. I'd already hired yacht designer Alan Andrews to contribute his ideas and skills to the

I had to trust in the experts. I knew I'd be adrift without them.

major structural work we intended to do. You don't take a boat apart, move stuff around, and then put it all back together like some sort of floating Humpty Dumpty without having all the king's good men gathered for the effort.

A graduate of Stanford University with a degree in mechanical engineering, Alan Andrews has been designing yachts since 1979. He specializes in designing high-performance racing and cruising sailboats.

Dennis Choate has likewise been a fixture in West Coast yacht design and building for decades. He got his start in 1973, and he's been going strong ever since. Diversified Composites is his latest venture. Both of these guys are Transpac heavies, having worked on numerous boats whose owners wanted their yachts retrofitted to be as fast as possible for a shot at a Transpac win. Alan and Dennis were both involved in the construction of the forty-eight-foot *Arriba,* which Dennis skippered to a win in the 1979 Transpac. He also was and still is active in the local racing circuit, and he was named Yachtsman of the Year by *One Design & Offshore Yachtsman* magazine (present-day *Sailing World*).

Dennis walked up to *Merlin* and tapped the hull with a small hammer. I knew he was listening for a dull, hollow sound that might indicate a saturated core. He evidently heard something he didn't like, and he brought the hole saw up and hit the trigger. The saw whirred. Little white-and-tan fiberglass shards twisted around the blade of the saw and fell to the concrete in a small pile topped with tawny wood shavings. A small circular hole appeared in *Merlin*'s side.

"I don't like drilling holes in a boat. Especially my boat," I said. "Seems counterintuitive."

Dennis laughed, dislodging the core sample from the hole saw. He held it up, sniffed it, examined it closely, felt it.

"Anything?" I asked, my anxiety rising.

"Looks good," he said, handing me the balsa disc. "Here. Check it out for yourself. Dry as a bone."

I took the sample and examined it, just as Dennis had, even though I wouldn't have known if there was a problem unless it jumped up and bit me on the nose. Of course, if the balsa was soaking wet, anyone with an ounce of brains could see that would pose a big problem. The smell of the core can tell you things, though, and so can the texture of the balsa, but you have to know what you're doing to really determine whether any structural integrity has been lost due to water ingress, flexing, stress, and other factors that come into play when you constantly push a boat to the max.

He took a few more samples. Fortunately, the core was dry. *Merlin* had passed an important test. Wet core can be remediated, but it's an expensive and time-consuming process. We were gearing up for the 2019 Transpac, slated for the following July. The yard had just done extensive work on a competitor, *Taxi Dancer*, and the job, which was similar in scope to ours, had taken about a year to complete. We didn't have time to mess around. I had to make the decisions, and I had to make them in a timely manner if Dennis and his crew were to have enough time to do the work. As it turned out, we were only able to squeeze four practice sessions in shortly before the race.

After we finished turning *Merlin* into swiss cheese, we climbed up the ladder situated at the stern and stepped into the cockpit. Brian and I had written down an action plan, revising and tweaking it after numerous discussions. I'd already approved the construction of a brand-new, lightweight carbon fiber mast that would stand eighty feet above the deck. Offshore Spars was also fabricating a new carbon fiber boom two feet shorter than the original one. The idea was to reduce *Merlin*'s tendency toward excessive heel when sailing to windward by slightly depowering the mainsail with a small reduction in sail area.

Of course, making the boom two feet shorter meant I'd have to have North Sails fabricate a brand-new mainsail. While we were at it, we also ordered a new A2 Rainbow Warrior spinnaker, a new blast reacher (a nonoverlapping headsail used for reaching), a new A4 headsail, and a new jib. Sails are the motor of a racing yacht. They are just as important for speed as a smooth, friction-free hull surface.

As we all stood there looking at the cockpit, I had the sinking feeling of having stepped in financial quicksand. As soon as you change one thing on a boat, you usually have to change something else. And all of that will cost money. Lots of money. Tons of money! I just didn't know how much at the time, because one thing definitely leads to another during a major retrofit. At least it did with me.

"You know, we can really open up the cockpit if we lose the traveler," Dennis said. Chris Watts had been saying the same thing for months.

In the current cockpit design, you had to step over the traveler mount, a vertical rise of fiberglass that sliced the cockpit into two sections. The traveler's block and tackle "traveled" on a track affixed to the top of the platform. To adjust sail trim with the traveler, you simply moved the fitting attached to the block and tackle from side to side on the track as needed.

In boats of *Merlin*'s age, that arrangement was the norm. Nowadays, many modern racing boats have internal travelers and mainsheets (lines used to control and trim the mainsail), and that's what we wanted. To compete against modern sleds, the retrofit of *Merlin*'s traveler was required. I was out to break *Merlin*'s old records for the Transpac, and I knew the boat would have to be brought up to modern standards to do it.

In addition, I wanted the primary winches moved forward to make room for new steering platforms. I prefer to sit on the high side to steer. I can see the sails better from there, but in the present cockpit I was practically sitting in Chris's lap when he was trimming the main. I told Dennis I loved the idea of removing the traveler mount. It would make room for a pair of steering platforms—flat seats attached to the stern rail where I could get a good view while driving the boat.

"You know, you really don't need all that cabin space," Dennis said. "If we cut off some of the cabin, we can make the cockpit longer to give the crew more room."

That suggestion launched us into a detailed discussion. Certainly, cutting two feet off the back end of the cabin would add more length to the cockpit, giving us room for the new carbon fiber "coffee grinder" and more space for steering and trimming. For nonsailors, a coffee grinder is a winch set on a vertical pole about four feet tall. Cranks protrude from the top of the mechanism. You literally crank it like a coffee grinder as you winch in the sails. We also discussed moving the primary winches forward about three feet to maximize the space for the pit crew.

We didn't know it at the time, but cutting off part of the cabin made *Merlin* wetter, more like she was when Bill had first launched her. Every action can have unintended consequences. We didn't mind that the boat had reverted to her wetter self. The lower cabin made it easier for us to walk fore and aft unencumbered, and the new soft nonskid we added forward made it safer and more comfortable when on the foredeck during sail changes.

After talking over the changes in the cockpit and deck layout, we went below to have a look around. The main goal of the retrofit was to make *Merlin* faster without radically changing her design and look. At one point, the suggestion of adding a second wheel came up. Most modern racers have two wheels, allowing the skipper to easily steer from the low or high side of the boat. I vetoed the suggestion because two wheels would make the boat look different, and I didn't want that. I wanted *Merlin* to be instantly recognizable as the venerable classic that she is.

The most important steps in achieving our goal for the boat were to reduce as much weight as possible and to move the majority of the weight to the center of the boat. It turned out that chopping two feet off the cabin would set other changes in motion as well.

Dennis thought for a moment and said, "You know, if you're going to make the cabin that much shorter, we can move the engine forward about eight feet, and we can install it under the new companionway stairs. That would get the weight out of the stern, and it would open up lots of cabin space aft."

Much has changed in marine engines since 1977. One significant development subsequent to *Merlin*'s launch was the invention of the saildrive. Basically, the system entails connecting an engine to the saildrive unit. It does not use a traditional shaft and propeller, thereby saving weight and drag. Instead, the saildrive extends down under the hull, and a "feathering prop" is attached to the drive. Feathering props open and close like flowers. When the engine is turned off and the boat is under sail, the forward momentum closes the prop. When the engine is turned on, the drive shaft spins the prop open.

Naturally, the question arose as to whether we should install a rebuild for $5,000, or just buy a new engine and saildrive for $20,000. I considered the entire project, and I decided it would be foolish to cut corners. We went for a new Yanmar diesel engine, and a new saildrive.

"So, if we're shortening the cabin and moving the engine forward," Dennis said, his enthusiasm increasing by the second, "then we can move the rudder forward by about seven feet. That'll move the wheel up as well."

Cha-ching! This trip is gonna be expensive, I thought.

"And we can put a kelp cutter on the rudder!" Dennis said.

Moving the rudder forward made sense. The rudder had the bad habit of sometimes breaking the surface of the water when *Merlin* was heeled way over on her side, and then we'd momentarily lose steering efficiency. It can be, well, *disconcerting* to feel the rudder go mushy when you're sailing full blast on a crowded racecourse where maneuverability can mean the difference between a collision or getting clear in the nick of time.

Additionally, moving the rudder forward would reduce drag from oversteering. Retrofitting a kelp cutter for the rudder was a good idea as well. A kelp cutter is a slender blade attached to the leading edge of the rudder or keel. You access it through a fitting on the deck, which allows you to slide the blade up and down to cut kelp that gets caught on the leading edge. With a straight vertical drop from the hull for both the rudder and keel, kelp can easily get stuck, adding drag and slowing the boat. You need the cutter to get it off.

Moving the rudder meant we'd need to design a new quadrant, the device used to turn the rudder post and gain mechanical advantage. The present system was aluminum and employed twelve feet of heavy stainless-steel cable.

"We can go with a carbon fiber build to save weight on the quadrant," Dennis said.

Cha-ching!

"And we can do a new carbon fiber wheel," Dennis said. "It won't save all that much weight, but every ounce does count."

Everything Dennis was saying made perfect sense. It was just that I wasn't prepared for the extent of the retrofit when I'd initially agreed that modernizing *Merlin* should not be done incrementally, but all at once. The project was getting much bigger than originally conceived.

Ultimately, I had to bite the bullet and make the decision to authorize the work. In the end, I'm glad I did, but the sticker shock was painful.

We found all kinds of ways to save weight by using carbon fiber for just about anything you can think of. The head (toilet) is carbon fiber, and so is the galley (kitchen) sink. We went with internal carbon fiber chain plates for the shrouds, and carbon fiber chain plates for the stays. We switched from heavy stainless-steel standing rigging to carbon fiber stays and shrouds, and we installed a carbon fiber mast step.

We felt it was vital to reduce as much weight as possible aloft. Heavy spars, fittings, and cables can exacerbate the motion of a boat. It's kind of like how the weight on the arm of a metronome moves the arm from side to side. Between the new carbon fiber mast and boom, and all the other changes we made, we shaved 425 pounds off the old rig.

Intent on saving weight wherever we could, we went through virtually every part of the boat to see where we could cut without sacrificing safety and efficiency. For example, we moved the battery bank forward to enhance hull trim. We replaced the lead-acid batteries with much lighter lithium-ion batteries, saving about 400 pounds. We even replaced the old sat-com dome with a carbon fiber one and saved another 125 pounds.

All this might not sound like much, but it is. Recall that the boat only displaces 24,000 pounds. Shaving off about a total of 950 pounds in weight is significant when you consider how light she already was.

The boat has been stripped down to the basics. We don't have a dining table. The galley is little more than a spartan place to heat up food, and the head crammed up forward in the bow doesn't even have a privacy curtain. You won't find creature comforts on an offshore racing sled. Each crew member gets a small cubby for personal gear, and that's it. We don't even have a full complement of dedicated berths. Some astern are more like hammocks. We have an efficient watermaker, so we don't have to carry excessive amounts of water. Water weighs eight pounds per gallon, after all.

The day spent with Dennis and Brian at Diversified Composites was a real eye-opener for me. I realized that owning a classic racing yacht was about more than just racing. I had a responsibility to preserve what Bill envisioned when he built *Merlin* in a chicken coop all those years ago, and yet I wanted to modernize the yacht to make her more competitive with newer boats. Everything, or almost everything, requires a sense of balance, an ability to see where to push or pull. I believed that I could modernize the boat with the help of Dennis and his crew without compromising Bill's design. By the end of the planning, I was confident that I'd achieved the balance I was looking for.

I flew home to Tampa, my head in a whirl about all that had to be done in a relatively short time. I had a superb program manager for Team *Merlin* in Brian. I had a top yacht designer in Alan Andrews. I had a great crew at Diversified Composites under the watchful and knowledgeable guidance of Dennis Choate.

In the end, success on the racecourse and in business depends entirely on the quality of the people around you. That was becoming clearer to me with each new adventure, and I knew we were all in for the biggest one yet when we ran *Merlin* in the 2019 Transpac.

> In the end, success on the racecourse and in business depends entirely on the quality of the people around you.

9

TRANSPAC

I TRIED NOT TO grip the wheel too hard, willing myself to stay cool as I eyeballed the nearest competitors in the fleet. I watched for puffs of light wind that would show as subtle dark ripples on the smooth gray water off Long Beach. When the wind picked up, I steered to get as much lift as possible to keep the boat moving among the crowd jockeying for position just before the starting line. Jeff Linton, tactician for the race, called the shots as we timed the start of the 2019 Transpac, the fiftieth running of this iconic race. I'd wanted to run in this particular race, as it was occurring on an important anniversary year for the event, and we'd made it, although just by the skin of our teeth.

The two waves of smaller boats had already left with good winds under sunny skies. Now it looked as if Division 2 would not be so lucky. The weather forecast for Saturday, July 13, 2019, predicted light southwesterly winds—not the ideal setup to break racecourse records.

Being on the starting line for the Transpac marked an important milestone for Team *Merlin*. It represented the accomplishment of a major goal for me and the boat, and the continuation of what I knew would be a never-ending learning curve when it came to offshore ocean racing. You never stop learning and honing your skills as a sailor. Like any worthwhile endeavor that nourishes the soul, it's an ongoing process.

If we're not learning and trying new things, stagnation can set in, both in our personal and work lives. Challenges stimulate the mind, and they encourage positive action to meet them head-on. In many ways, people are like sharks. We always have to keep moving if we want to live.

We had several goals to achieve by the end of the race. The first was to win the Barn Door Trophy, given to the first monohull to finish. We doubted we'd win it, not with the likes of the one-hundred-foot *Comanche* and the ninety-nine-foot *Rio* as competitors, but we could always hope. Wind and sea conditions can vary greatly, depending on where you are at any given time on the racecourse. A yacht one hundred miles away can catch a bad break, while everything goes well for you. For example, we enviously knew that the first two waves of the ninety boats that had started the race were sailing happily along in good air as the northeast trades clocked around to give them the downwind race that the Transpac is famous for.

The next goal was to finish first in our division, a definite possibility, though we were rated as the fastest boat and would therefore have to beat significant time allowances given to the other competitors in our division. We could finish first in Division 2 and still lose out on line honors. We'd set a course record in the Mexico race in 2018, and yet we still lost the race in our class on corrected time due to the handicap rules. The Transpac is more complicated than most other handicap races because the handicapping is in part calculated based on average wind speeds for each quadrant of the race. That meant that even more variables could come into play to determine the winner's corrected time.

On a personal level, I wanted to beat *Merlin*'s record that Bill Lee had set in the 2017 Transpac with an elapsed time of eight days, two hours, thirty-four minutes, and nine seconds. The icing on the cake would be if we could blow into Diamond Head in under eight days. In her storied career, *Merlin* hadn't done that yet.

Navigator Adrienne Cahalan called time and distance off. We were between halfway and a third of the way down the line. The fleet stretched out on either side of us, the primarily black carbon fiber sails creating a sea of triangular mains and headsails atop sleek colorful hulls that contrasted with the grayness of the water and clouds. "Four minutes to start!" she said.

I noted that the wind had dropped slightly, slowing us down. "Man, we should get closer to the line," I said. "We're too far out."

"Not too close," Jeff said. "We don't want to jam ourselves up."

Before I could answer, the water off to port darkened as a stronger puff approached. The wind increased, *Merlin* took off, and we were fast running into the wrong spot in the fleet.

"Ready about?" I said loudly to alert the pit crew.

"Ready about," the pit crew replied.

"Helm's alee," I said, tacking the boat around with the hope of finding the sweet spot in the fleet.

The wind increased still more, and the action started happening fast. We were too far down the line, and we were getting boxed in among the largest and fastest yachts in the fleet. The maxi yacht *Comanche* tacked and screamed up on us like a rocket, her red bow slicing through the water. With her 150-foot mast, twenty-five-foot beam (her nickname is the "aircraft carrier" because she's so wide), and a draft of twenty-one feet, she dwarfed *Merlin*. If she got much closer, she'd blanket us completely, stopping us dead in her wind shadow. If that happened, we'd lose precious time that could mean the difference between winning or losing in our division of eight boats. *Rio* was also nearby on the line. I felt like we'd wandered into the wrong neighborhood, and in fact we had.

"Thirty seconds!" Adrienne said.

Comanche was about to eat our lunch. *Great, just what we need,* I thought. *Of all the bonehead moves to make.*

I didn't need Jeff to tell me we were running out of room. We were bearing down on the committee boat.

"Twenty seconds!"

I took a deep breath, praying we wouldn't overshoot. I clearly saw the guy at the starting gun staring straight at me, an expression on his face that said, "Are you nuts?"

"Ten seconds!"

This is gonna be tight! I thought.

Kaboom!

The cannon fired just as we crossed the starting line. The crew whooped, laughed, and gave each other the thumbs-up.

"Way to go, Jeff! That was one hell of a start!" I said, shooting Jeff a big smile to say the hairy start had turned out okay in the end.

Brian Malone sighed and glanced aft. "Yeah, perfect for about thirty seconds, because look at what's coming."

Comanche sailed to weather of us, and I worried once again about being blanketed. Then she fell off to leeward and sped away on the steady light breeze, only slowing us a little in the dirty air she left in her wake. The other one-hundred-footer, *Rio*, blasted along to weather of us without much harm.

We concentrated on the sails, the wind angle, and the other boats in our effort to find the clear air I was looking for. The southerly wind held, for the moment anyway, and we quickly moved out to the front of the fleet into clear air. The bigger boats kept the lead, but we maintained a good pace that made me think—no, fervently hope—that the weather report predicting light air was wrong.

About six months before the race, Brian and I had attended a class run by Stan Honey, who's considered among the best navigators in the world. One of his navigating gigs was aboard *Comanche*. He'd walked the class through what we could expect in terms of weather, wind, and sea conditions, and he spent a great deal of time discussing race tactics. One of the key points he made was that we had to get past Catalina Island on the first day. Typically, you beat out to the Channel Islands past Catalina, and then bear off south-southwest to sail along the southeast edge of the Pacific High to pick up the northeast trade winds. The trick is to get into the trades as fast as possible, so clearing Catalina quickly is the first big step.

"If you don't get past Catalina Island on the first day, you might as well pack it in. It won't be a fast Transpac for you," Stan said.

His words echoed in my mind as I watched the wind speed steadily decline as the afternoon progressed and we began a long, slow crawl southwest to Catalina Island. We were caught in the notorious Catalina Eddy, a vortex of dead air that had becalmed the fleet. My frustration mounted as the sea became an expanse of glassy low groundswells rolling in from the Pacific.

While Stan may have proclaimed our race doomed from the start because of the delay in getting away from the coast and out into the northeast trades, I felt determined not to give up, despite my annoyance about the lack of wind. Quitting would be worse than sitting around waiting for a breeze. Some boats in the first two waves were experiencing problems and had to turn back, and I felt badly for the skippers and crews on those boats. A lot of time, money, and emotion gets invested when you participate in a race like the Transpac.

Earlier in the morning, at about 6:30 a.m., the Beneteau First 47.7 *Macondo* retired from the race, citing rudder trouble. The boat's owner, Mike Sudo, had spent more than two years doing extensive work to make *Macondo* as competitive as possible, and turning back was not an easy decision for him or the crew. Kyle R. Clement, a.k.a. K2 on the boat's blog, wrote about the disappointment he and the rest of the crew felt about retiring from the race:

> Punch to the gut? Of course. I seem to find never-ending parallels in sailing and life, and today is no different. Sometimes elements are purely out of your control; however, you can control how you react and control the next move. The decision to turn back was to subconsciously strip us all down to the nerves and decide there are more important things than winning or finishing, champagne showers or celebratory social media posts, and it's these realizations we seek when we leave safe harbor in the first damn place ... These are the reminders that hopefully make us better sailors, better people. We don't do this to win or to conquer nature; we do this to somehow remind ourselves we are nature, that we're still wild, a part of it all, and to marvel in its splendor.

I understood that I had no power to control the wind, and that I did have the power to control how I reacted to the situation, but I just lost my patience. Fuming, I turned to Jeff and said, "Here, you take over. I can't take this crap anymore."

Jeff nodded, took the wheel, and patiently coaxed *Merlin* to move whenever a puff blessed us with its presence. I don't know where he got the patience to sail like that. I just knew he was much, much better at light-air sailing than I would ever be. If there's no wind, I'd rather do something else, like go to work on a fascinating legal case. Jeff and the pit crew kept at it. We'd coast a short way, and then stop. Coast. Stop. Coast. Stop. I could get out and walk faster than the boat was going. Yet we drew closer and closer to *Comanche* and *Rio* with each tack.

"Holy cow!" I said. "We're catching up to *Comanche*!"

And we were ... at a rip-tearing two knots. In the current conditions, size didn't matter as much as weight. The lighter boats had the advantage, such as it was. We continued to ghost along, but *Comanche* and *Rio* kept the lead. It would have been lots of fun to have overtaken either boat.

While the fleet had begun to scatter, we could still see many of our competitors, which motivated us to keep pushing hard. It's more difficult to stay motivated when you're all alone, and your competitors are blips on the computer tracking app. But if you can see them and visually mark your progress (or lack thereof) against them—well, that's going to light a fire under you, or at least it should light one. There's no room for complacency on a racecourse or in a boardroom.

> There's no room for complacency on a racecourse or in a boardroom.

The first night passed in slow-motion torture. It didn't take a rocket scientist to see that the spirits of the crew were not as high as they should have been. The constant motion and boredom started to wear us down. We rolled, sloshed, banged, clanged, and pitched for much of the night under an overcast sky that blotted out the stars. We sailed, stopped, and sailed on. Everything on deck was blackness as we rolled around in the low swells, the mainsail going slack and then filling with a loud boom.

Shivering in the cold, the on-watch crew turned on miner's-style headlamps fitted with red light bulbs to prevent the night blindness that occurs when you look at a bright white light. It was like sailing into the abyss. In some ways, being out in the ocean in the darkness was almost like experiencing a session in a sensory-deprivation tank. You separate yourself from reality. Your thoughts wander. You feel a primal connection to the universe that you just don't get when you sit home watching TV.

When dawn on Sunday morning finally arrived, we'd only traveled roughly sixty miles of the 2,225-mile-long voyage. The rest of our fleet fared about the same as we did. The clouds lifted, and the beauty of the sunrise captivated me as I watched the sky lighten to the east. Soon the sun's rays painted the waves a light orange that changed gradually to the deep navy blue of the open ocean. The wind increased a little, and our spirits rose a lot as the boat began to move more quickly through the swells. The wind pressure against the sails helped smooth out the jerky seesaw motion of the boat, a real bonus for us all.

The tracker app showed how our fleet was steadily spreading out. Each skipper decided which way to go, either north or south of the suggested course to Oahu. We chose to head farther south than almost any other boat. Most stayed bunched up farther north and on a more westerly heading, still south of the rhumb line.

We were hoping to pick up more wind lower down, and to avoid the dead air in a high-pressure system that sat to the north. We were playing the classic slot tactics, weighing whether we should add distance sailed in favor of better wind angles, or whether we should accept a less efficient wind angle in favor of a more direct route to Diamond Head. In a sense, we split the difference. We adjusted course to a slightly more westerly slant, putting us on a very tight close reach. Once the wind clocked around a bit more, we'd be able to fly a spinnaker and really get going on our way.

I could see that the crew worked well together. We had a good mix of personalities, and we had decades of collective offshore racing experience to draw on. Many of the ten crew members were old *Merlin* vets, and the new members were all top-flight sailors with plenty of racing chops to bring to the party. I knew that if—or, more probably, *when*—the fur hit the fan, we'd be ready for just about anything that came our way. Unlike in previous races, we'd been able to practice more extensively together before the big day.

As I sat pondering the big blue sea, I thought back on our four practice sessions. We'd motored out of Alamitos Bay Marina, navigating the traffic in the channel. With a draft of eleven feet, we had to stay right in the center. Kids taking sailing lessons, boats coming and going from the many marinas, people ashore at the restaurants overlooking the water—it all made for a festive setting as race day approached. Outside the yacht basin, we still weren't in the open ocean. Los Angeles and Long Beach Harbors are hemmed in with a massive breakwater. Oil derricks still pump oil just offshore, and the derricks are disguised as islands for cosmetic reasons.

We cruised over to one of the faux isles, got in its lee, and tried to figure out how to put the new mainsail up. It took us fifteen minutes (we can do it in five now). In many ways, that first session was like stepping aboard a new boat for all of us. In fact, Dennis had sent over one of the expert craftsmen who worked on the retrofit to give us a quick tutorial on how to baby carbon fiber. The material is light and strong, but it can also break easily when subjected to pressure in the wrong place. For example, we were told to never tie anything to the spreaders because the tension on the extrusion could break it, and yet the spreaders could stand up to tremendous loads. It seemed like a paradox to me. How could something so strong be so potentially weak at the same time?

We went over how everything worked, and then we got the sails up. I glanced over at Chris as the boat accelerated.

"Notice a difference?" I asked.

Chris beamed. "Awesome! She's like a new *Merlin*!"

And she was. I felt a difference in the helm. The touch was lighter, if that was even possible. The open cockpit with the new coffee grinder was much easier to work in. The new deck organizer fed the lines back to the winches more efficiently. The new nonskid was soft underfoot. I smiled as we put *Merlin* through her paces, practicing sail changes and sail handling on all points of sail. We sailed in a variety of conditions, even getting lucky with a twenty-plus-knot breeze.

As we adjusted the sails for optimal trim, we used a black Sharpie to mark the sheets so that we could instantly trim the sail without guessing. You just winch the sheet in or ease it out to reach the black line that matches your point of sail as well as wind speed, and you're good to go. Marking the sheets saves seconds when you're in a tacking duel with another boat. The only problem was we foolishly used a black Sharpie, so it was tough to see the marks at night. We vowed to use a fluorescent marker the next time.

Much of the practice involved tuning the boat. How do you get the perfect foil? Under what wind conditions? Sailors know you can change the shape of a sail in any number of ways to maximize its shape efficiency. A mainsail's shape can be tweaked with the boom vang, the traveler, the halyard, and the backstay. Essentially, you can either flatten the sail, or you can make it fuller. In light air, you want a fuller main. In heavy air, you flatten the main out to depower it somewhat to keep the boat sailing on its keel, not on its side. We learned a lot during those practice sessions, and we were still learning. I just couldn't wait to see what *Merlin* would do when we got into the trade winds.

Fortunately, the wind continued to increase during the second day of the race. We also got better wind angles the farther out we sailed. Up went the Rainbow Warrior, and we quickly were making well over ten knots and pulling ahead in our division, battling it out with *Taxi Dancer* as we repeatedly switched positions.

On the radio check-ins that are part of the race, we heard about more damage sustained by the fleet. At about 9:30 p.m., *Maserati*, a MOD 70 trimaran owned by Giovanni Soldini, was sailing at about twenty-four knots when the crew heard a tremendous bang on the left-hand hull and then felt the boat violently shudder. All hands rushed on deck as a grinding sound ripped along the side of the hull. Another loud bang followed a second later as the object slammed into the rudder. The yacht had collided with a large floating object about three feet high. In the darkness, the crew couldn't see what the object was, only that it was big enough to have damaged the yacht's hull and rudder.

I knew from our own experience off Bermuda that not all shipping containers sink after getting washed overboard. Some float, with most of the mass remaining submerged, much like an iceberg. Consider some numbers. A typical twenty-foot shipping container is roughly eight feet wide and a little over eight feet high. Empty, the thing weighs more than two tons. For big loads, shippers use the forty-foot containers. Those weigh more than nine thousand pounds when they're empty. Who knows what the container would weigh if it was fully loaded. As you can see, smacking into a shipping container while sailing at more than twenty knots can send you to the bottom in a matter of minutes. It's a little like sailing full bore into a brick wall.

Did *Maserati* hit a shipping container? We'll never know for sure, but it seems likely to me that she did. The crew jury-rigged the rudder and kept on going, eventually finishing the race.

Later that night, at two a.m., race headquarters received a report from *OEX*, an Andrews 70 designed and built by Bill Lee, saying they were taking on water. Skipper John Sangmeister later said they were sailing fast when they suddenly heard a loud bang. They'd lost the rudder, and the boat was sinking fast. After putting out a Mayday, the crew deployed the life rafts and abandoned ship. The crew aboard the venerable Andrews 70 *Pyewacket* heard the call and responded, picking up the nine members of *OEX*'s crew at about three a.m.

Pyewacket is no stranger to the Transpac, and it's fitting that she was the one to rescue *OEX*'s crew. Back in 1975, Roy E. Disney, nephew of Walt Disney, sailed his first Transpac. He clearly loved the experience because he went on to sail in fourteen more races, the last of which was in 2005. He did the race in a number of different boats, but he eventually settled on a series of four yachts that he named *Pyewacket*. Pyewacket was the name of the witch's Siamese cat in the 1958 movie *Bell, Book and Candle*. Walt Disney did not produce the film.

The second *Pyewacket*, a Turbo 70, broke *Merlin*'s twenty-year Transpac record in 1997 when she won the Barn Door Trophy with an elapsed time of seven days, fifteen hours, twenty-four minutes, and forty seconds. By comparison, *Merlin* did the 1997 race in eight days, three hours. Roy E. Disney didn't participate in the race due to a broken leg suffered in a bad car accident. His son, Roy Pat, skippered the yacht.

In 1999, during the fortieth running of the Transpac, Roy E. Disney set a new record with the third *Pyewacket*, a Reichel/Pugh 73 maxi yacht, beating his son's record by three and three-quarters of an hour with an elapsed time of seven days, eleven hours, forty-one minutes, and twenty-seven seconds. The 1999 race was atypical, in that the usual trade winds didn't materialize. The race was upwind all the way. In fact, *Pyewacket*'s skipper said they didn't have the spinnaker up once, which was very unusual in a Transpac. *Pyewacket* setting a new course record under those circumstances remains an impressive demonstration of seamanship, sail handling, and racing tactics.

We heard about *OEX* at about eight o'clock on Monday morning, when Adrienne relayed our position report to race headquarters. When she got the news, she gasped and shouted, "Oh, my God! *OEX* sank last night!"

"What?" I asked, hurrying to the nav station.

"*OEX* is lost. All crew safe. *Pyewacket* picked them up," she said.

"What happened?" I asked.

"They think it was rudder failure."

The mood aboard went somber. The sinking reminded us all about how dangerous and unforgiving the ocean could be. It seemed surreal that *OEX*, which had been docked next to *Merlin* a few days earlier, could have sunk. I imagined what it must have been like to hear the torrents of water flowing into the boat, and seeing it rise in the dim red light of the nav station. I imagined the utter horror of it as the crew realized that they were sinking, and sinking fast. I wondered what it was like to step into a life raft in the darkness with only the stars above and the vast black ocean heaving around me. I still get chills when I think about it, but the crew was safe, and that was all that mattered. You can always replace a boat; you can't replace a life.

> I wondered what it was like to step into a life raft in the darkness with only the stars above and the vast black ocean heaving around me.

"I think we should check our rudder," I said.

We did. It was fine. We checked it often after we'd heard what had happened to *OEX*. Later, we found out that five of the eight boats that retired had done so because of some sort of rudder problem. It's part of the challenge of the Transpac that the fleet often sails on a long reach to Hawaii, which can produce enough stress on a rudder to find its breaking point. Additionally, one boat withdrew due to water ingress, and one suffered a broken mast. *Pyewacket* withdrew from the race to rescue the crew of *OEX*.

We were now well into the northeast trades. Our position report on July 16, our fourth day at sea, put us 526 nautical miles from Long Beach, and fourth in Division 2 on corrected time, despite the fact that we were way out in front of the division in terms of our actual position. We'd sailed 274 nautical miles in one twenty-four-hour period. *Merlin* could do much better, but the run was still good. It definitely beat sitting still off Catalina Island.

At day four, we celebrated reaching the halfway point to Oahu. Yes, we still had more than half the mileage to cover. Based on *Merlin's* previous Transpac passages, however, she consistently completed the race in just over eight days. It was a pretty safe bet that she'd do it again. As I said, we really wanted to arrive at Diamond Head in seven days or so. That didn't look like it was going to happen because of the slow start.

The farther out we sailed, the better the wind conditions were for optimal speed. We routinely surfed ten-foot seas at an average of about thirteen knots. We vied for the lead in corrected time with *Taxi Dancer* and *Buona Sera*. We'd pull ahead, and then *Taxi Dancer* would catch up and pass us on corrected time. We were physically ahead, but *Taxi Dancer* could still beat us because of the handicap rules.

I'd never sailed in seas like the ones I encountered on the passage to Hawaii. The long rollers looked like blue hills. They were big enough for *Merlin* to sit on and ride. She rolled her spinnaker pole down toward the water, and then she rolled over the other way to threaten to dip the boom. You can break something if you dip a spar, so the idea is to push the boat to the limits of safety without crossing that line.

In addition to the wind-driven swells, we dealt with a nasty cross sea for much of the voyage, with one wave train colliding with another one from an oblique angle. When the waves behind us broke, white water boiled around the cockpit, and green solid water swept from bow to stern, reenacting *Merlin*'s famous "cosmic flush." The turbulent seas made it tough to keep the spinnaker full. If the boat hit a cross sea just right, she'd literally whack the air out of the spinnaker, causing it to partially collapse, only to fill again a second later with a thunderous boom. The entire rig shook when that happened. Obviously, the person at the helm tried to keep the chute full at all times. It wasn't easy in those conditions.

The wind increased to more than twenty knots, and *Merlin* simply flew through the water. It gave me a feeling of pride and a sense of deep satisfaction to be out there in the middle of the ocean with a great boat, a superb crew, and weather conditions that would have made Bill Lee smile. We kept up the pressure on us and the boat, not relaxing for even a second while we were on watch.

The constant motion, the lack of sleep, the bruises, the fighting to move when the boat was steeply heeled, the eating just for body fuel, all these realities of shipboard life on a racing boat tend

> The ocean has a way of doing that, bringing sailors together for the accomplishment of a shared mission—getting to safe harbor in one piece.

to wear you out on a long passage. Yet the adversity creates a bond between you and your shipmates that cannot be equaled anywhere else. The ocean has a way of doing that, bringing sailors together for the accomplishment of a shared mission—getting to safe harbor in one piece.

July 17, or day five, ushered in strong winds and black squalls. The ocean appeared dark gray, almost black, under the overcast sky. High winds aloft sent clouds racing above us. The weather was warm, which was pleasant enough, but the sea and sky looked ominous, almost malevolent. Adrienne tried her best to navigate us around the squalls, and we largely succeeded. If we stumbled into a bad one, we'd have to reduce sail, and we certainly didn't want to do that!

Shortly after sunset, we had the big Rainbow Warrior up. *Merlin* flew through the dark seas, and it gave me a strange sensation, as if I were hurtling through space into an endless void. The wind was right at the edge of the sail's limit, at around twenty knots. I wondered if we should douse the Rainbow Warrior and put up a smaller spinnaker, but I figured the risk was worth it for the extra speed. The big spinnakers are the workhorses of the Transpac. I wanted to use ours as much as possible.

"Hey, guys," I said, "looks like everything's fine. I'm going below for some shut-eye."

I stepped into the companionway …

Kaboom!

In a matter of seconds, the Rainbow Warrior blew apart.

Uh-oh, I thought as I popped my head out of the companionway, jaw momentarily agape at what I was seeing. We all moved swiftly to douse the sail and set another spinnaker, Brian all the while lamenting the blowout. North Sails had made the new chute for us, and we'd wanted to fly it as we roared toward the finish line off Diamond Head.

It was a colorful sail that would have looked great in the videos of the finish.

After the race, we learned that several boats in our division had also blown out their big kites. The combination of fresh winds and a nasty cross sea had made it challenging to fly the big A2 spinnakers. We were clearly not the only ones to have had trouble.

At this point, we led our division in terms of position, but we had fallen to third place on corrected time. *Taxi Dancer* battled *Buona Sera* for the lead on corrected time, and we continued to give both yachts a run for their money. We spent the rest of July 17 setting and dousing spinnakers.

The weather cleared on day six, and that night we sailed beneath stars that filled the sky with faint white points of light. The Milky Way had never been clearer to me. The heavens are spectacular when you don't have any light pollution to mar the scene. The moon rose, and a white halo formed around it to make a moonbow. My memory of the beauty of that night will remain with me for the rest of my life.

We made steady progress, putting mile after mile between ourselves and the rest of the boats in our division, but we were still not pulling ahead on corrected time. The strange handicap rules were hard on *Merlin*, especially when factoring average wind speeds in the four quadrants of the racecourse into the equation. I'm not saying that the deck was stacked against us, but I am saying we had to work extra hard to win on corrected time, no matter what race we were in. *Merlin*'s design means she's going to get a fast rating, and that's just the way it is.

On day seven, we were about twenty-four hours out of Oahu. Excitement aboard grew as we sailed closer and closer to Hawaii. On the morning of July 21, we were within sight of Molokai. I steered the boat to within half a mile of the island and craned my neck to look up at the majestic cliffs, their tawny heights topped with green. I felt a deep sense of emotion, as if something in me had changed, and it had. I was more confident in my sailing abilities, in the boat, and in the crew than ever. I was more in tune with my emotions, and with myself as a small part of the larger human condition.

I brought *Merlin* around for her final run to Diamond Head under full sail, including the Rainbow Warrior, which we had worked long and hard to repair during our off-watches. By early afternoon, we were closing in on the finish line. Helicopters flew overhead. Spectator boats milled about. I could only imagine the leis, rum punch, and a soft bed to sleep in as we roared in with a white rooster tail off the stern.

"Only eight minutes out," Adrienne said.

"Got it," I said, focusing on the sails.

Kaboom!

One minute everything was fine, and seconds later we had a problem. The spinnaker pole had snapped in two, causing the chute to flog. The noise was incredible. The pole had been giving us constant trouble throughout the entire voyage, and now, just minutes from the finish line, it came to a fitting end. I almost applauded. That pole had been the bane of all of us for most of the voyage, what with the fitting at the end of the pole letting go when least expected, causing us to look lively to get the sail back under control. The bow crew managed to tame the chute and rig it to the bowsprit for the final run in.

"One minute!" Adrienne shouted.

Everyone was silent, intent on his or her job.

"Fifteen seconds!"

Oh, God! I thought. *We really did it!*

And then we crossed the finish line at 1:32 p.m. We all cheered, hugged, high-fived, and thumbs-upped in our elation. Relief flooded over me. I felt the stress lift as we came into Honolulu. The hard work of racing on a passage of 2,382 nautical miles was over, and the celebrating would soon begin.

We finished first in our division, with an elapsed time of eight days, three hours, thirty-two minutes, and fourteen seconds, besting *Merlin*'s 1977 record by more than seven hours. We were one hour behind the time Bill Lee had set in 2017. We placed third in our division on corrected time. *Taxi Dancer* won, and *Bueno Sara* placed second.

"Well," I said to the pit crew, "we didn't make it in under seven days as we'd hoped, but we did good. Real good!"

We hadn't even arrived at our slip, and I was already hatching plans for the 2020 racing season. The offshore racing bug bit me hard in 2017 when, on a lark, I sailed the Cuba race with Dave Kilcoyne aboard the good ship *Patience* and unwittingly opened an exciting new chapter in my life. So much had happened since then, and it had been quite a wild ride. Yet I knew I'd become part of something bigger than just me. I'd joined a community of offshore sailors, and I'd taken over stewardship of one of America's iconic racing yachts, a vessel whose design literally changed offshore sailboat racing. As we motored into Honolulu Harbor, I had the exhilarating sense that *Merlin*'s adventures were only just beginning.

APPENDIX

NO SKIPPER OR CEO can triumph without a great team. We had some fantastic individuals and companies working with us to make the 2018 and 2019 racing seasons a success. Below are some of the key players and crew lists for each of the races covered in this book.

Sailmaker: Brian Malone, North Sails Gulf Coast
Sail designer: Steve Reed, North Sails Design
Sail service: North Sails Chicago, North Sails Rhode Island, North Sails San Diego

RETROFIT

Dennis Choate, Diversified Composites
     Primary contractors: Charlie Escobedo, Duane Prichardson

Jimmy Slaughter, Pure Attitude Racing
     Project management, rigging, hardware design and fabrication

Alan Andrews, Andrews Yacht Design
     Design and engineering of offshore spars, spar builder

Doug Grant, Vang Master/Marine Products Engineering
     Custom machining and fabricating for the boom vang

Tim Pyne and James Tandy, Joule Yacht Transport

MERLIN CREW

<u>St. Petersburg to Habana 2018</u>

Chip Merlin

Brian Malone

Kat Malone

David Kilcoyne

Chris Watts

James Clappier

Mark Liebel

Kuli Vulinchenko

Neal Burns

Dan "Big Country" Peckham

Ben Givens

<u>St. Petersburg to Isla Mujeres 2018</u>

Chip Merlin

Brian Malone

Chris Watts

James Clappier

Dan "Big Country" Peckham

Kuli Vulinchenko

Lin Robson

Scott Macgregor

Joe Goulet

Cody Spruce

Mike Walbolt

<u>Newport to Bermuda 2018</u>

Chip Merlin

Bill Merlin

Brian Malone

Kat Malone

Chris Watts

David Kilcoyne

Keahi Ho

James Clappier

Chris Museler

Joe Goulet

Lin Robson

Dave German

Davey Arata

Kuli Vulinchenko

Chicago Mackinac 2018

Chip Merlin

Brian Malone

Kat Malone

Chris Watts

David Kilcoyne

Sarah Renz

Mark Renz

Keahi Ho

James Clappier

Dan "Big Country" Peckham

Joe Goulet

Verve Cup 2018

Chip Merlin

Brian Malone

Chris Watts

Keahi Ho

Trevor Baylis

Sarah Renz

Cam Warner

James Clappier

Ryan Kern

Orlando Montalvan

Patrick McMath

Matt Wachowicz

Grant Dumas

Joe Fanelli

Ben Bardwell

Peter Crawford

Joe Goulet

Transpac 2019

Chip Merlin

Brian Malone

Kat Malone

Jeff Linton

James Clappier

Chris Watts

Adrienne Cahalan

Mike Pentacost

Keahi Ho

Mackenzie Cook

ACKNOWLEDGMENTS

I WANT TO ACKNOWLEDGE Donice Krueger for her loving help and encouragement while writing this book, as well as all my family who have encouraged me to sail and have helped me on this venture, including Bill and Alice Merlin, my children Chase and Austin Merlin, my sisters Emily Merlin and Mary Alice Floyd, and Kim Merlin.

To the attorneys, management, and staff of Merlin Law Group, who dedicate themselves to helping policyholders in their time of need and who provided stories and support for this book: there would be little reason to write this book if not for the dreams and hope they provide to so many. I would like to especially thank Keona Williams, Eunice Elias, Catherine Finkenstadt, Justin Gregory, and Megan Conison for their help on this project and their work with Merlin.

The management and care for *Merlin* belongs to Brian and Kat Malone—they are making the dream of *Merlin* a reality. Bill Lee and Lu Lee have always been generous to us with their humble and gracious support and advice.

While the crew members on *Merlin*'s races since I purchased her are noted in an appendix, a special thanks is due to Chris Watts, who has been a fixture on *Merlin* since the day I was first aboard, and to

Hawaiian sailor Keahi Ho, who epitomizes the love so many have for this very special yacht.

Thanks to the prior owners of *Merlin* and their families, who have been so generous with sharing the history and stories of *Merlin*, including Bill Lee and Lu Lee, Don Campion, Al Micalief, the Orange Coast College School of Sailing and Seamanship, Trisha Steele, and the late Jere Sullivan.

Thanks to members and officers of yacht clubs where *Merlin* has found a berth since I have owned her, especially the St. Petersburg Yacht Club, the Hemingway Marina, the Newport Yacht Club, Royal Bermuda Yacht Club, the Chicago Yacht Club, the Long Beach Yacht Club, the Hawaiian Yacht Club, the Santa Cruz Yacht Club, and the St. Francis Yacht Club.

Thanks to the publishers and staff of Advantage, especially David Shaw, who was the architect and brains behind how this was all put together. Thanks also to my brilliant friend Amy Linton for her edits and suggestions.

Thanks to all those who make the sails for *Merlin* and who have worked on the rigging and equipment of *Merlin*, especially on the retrofit, including in particular sailmaker Brian Malone from North Sails Gulf Coast; sail designer Steve Reed of North Sails; the North Sails service crews from Chicago, Rhode Island, and San Diego; Dennis Choate and his staff from Diversified Composites; Charlie Escobedo; Duane Prichardson; Jimmy Slaughter of Pure Attitude Racing; Alan Andrews of Andrews Yacht Design; all those from Offshore Spars who built the mast and boom; Doug Grant of Vangmaster; a big shout out to James Clappier for his rigging; Mackenzie Cook; Dan "Big Country" Peckham; and Trevor Baylis.

Thanks to the editors of *Sail* magazine and especially sailing journalist Chris Museler for his article about *Merlin*. Thanks to the renowned sailing photographer Sharon Green and to everyone who has shared their photos and videos of *Merlin* so that a visual history of Merlin can be enjoyed by all. Thanks also to Ronnie Simpson, Snapshot Productions, and Sean German for making recent sailing videos of *Merlin*.

Thanks to all current and former competitors in the Sled Class who make the stories of Merlin so rich and endearing, especially Roy E. Disney, Roy P. Disney, Harry Moloscho, Bob McNulty, Peter Isler, Robbie Haines, Mike Campbell, Ed Marez, David Clark, David Happ, John Sangmeister, Doug Pasnik, Tom Parker, Jim Yabsley, Dick Compton, Mary Compton, Joe Crumm, Dale Williams, Ed and James McDowell, Bob Lane, Doug Ayres, Al and Vicki Schultz, Paul Sharp, Mitch Rouse, Lorenzo Berho, Brack Duker, Chris Slagerman, John DeLaura, Joel Ronning, Jim Ryley, Skip Allan, Paul Simonsen, John Kostecki, Jack Halterman, Zan Drejes, Morgan Larson, Carl Buchan, Mike Holt, Dee Smith, Stuart Kett, Don and Susie Snyder, Dave Wahle, Peter Tong, John Jourdane, Dave Ulmann, Don Ayers, Nick Frazee, Doug Baker, Dick Pennington, John Landon, Peter Wilson, Fred and Steve Howe, Lance Smothermen, Burt D'Otterio, Bill and Sally Martin, Stuart Dahlgren, John Nedeau, Mike Brotz, Terry Kohler, Peter Reicheledorfer, Paul LaMarche, Steve and Barb Schmidt, Jim Beauregard, Charles Canfield, Bill Martin, Charles Bayer, Chris Saxton, Bill Alcott, Brien Baker, and Mike Webb.

Thanks to my friends in the Gulf Yachting Association and at the Bay Waveland, St. Andrews Bay, and National Yacht Clubs, who raced with and against me during my formative yacht racing years and made me a lifelong lover of this crazy sport, including the Chapman, Egan, and Stieffel families; Hunter Riddle; William and Leslie Weatherly; Gail Murphy Hausler; Buzzy Hausler; Randy Santa Cruz; the Charles Wesley family; Mike Douglas; Duncan McClane; Chuck Barnes; Jill

Barnes; Ellen, Anne, and Maureen McBride; Evelyn Hamm; Rick Johnston; Cal Warriner; Lea Jackson; Dow Hutchison; George Haynie; the late Floyd Davis; John Morrow; James Fisher; Kenny Allen; David Holt; Chris Hamm; Leslie Laird; and Billie Mason.

Thanks to all the Flying Scot Sailing Association owners and members, especially former Flying Scot sailor Tom Ehman for all his promotion of yacht racing.

Finally, thanks to *Sports Illustrated* and journalist Richard W. Johnston, who captured the imagination and inspired a dream of a nineteen-year-old boy about a racing yacht designed by a wizard.

PHOTO GALLERY

Bill and Chip Merlin before the Start of Newport to Bermuda 2018

Chip Merlin and Donice Krueger with Merlin's *Trophies*
2018 St. Petersburg to Isla Mujeres Race

Merlin *Crew Celebrating the 2019 Transpac Finish*

2019 Transpac Finishers Party—Bill Lee and Chip Merlin

Chip Merlin with Lu and Bill Lee Post 2019 Transpac Party

2018 Chicago to Mackinac Prerace Crew Photo

2018 Line Honors and Course Record St. Petersburg to Isla Mujeres

Line Honors and First on Corrected Time in 2018 St. Petersburg to Havana

David Kilcoyne Holding Trophy Won by Patience *2017*
St. Petersburg to Havana Awards Ceremony

San Francisco Rolex Big Boat Race 2019

Merlin *Crew and Friends in Bermuda 2018*

2019 Transpac Finishers Party—Chip, Bill Lee, Chase Merlin

Merlin *Dwarfed by* Rio *and* Comanche *Shortly after Start of 2019 Transpac*

*Alice Merlin Receives Kisses from Bill and Chip
during Festivities after the 2018 Newport to Bermuda Race*